47 truths

Musings of a Modern-Day Multi-Medium Storyteller; A playful exploration of alchemy, coherence, and the transformational magic of words.

by Gabrielle Angel Dee Lilly, MA

Gabrielle Angel Dee Lilly

47 truths
Musings of a Modern-Day Multi-Medium Storyteller; A playful exploration of alchemy, coherence, and the transformational magic of words.

By Gabrielle Angel Dee Lilly, M.A.
First Edition, December 31, 2018

GAL Media & BlueRavenBooks

Paperback Edition
Copyright: January 7, 2019

A FunFast Production

ISBN: 978-1-7326698-8-8

Gabrielle Angel Dee Lilly

"Parts of Me"
~Angel Lilly, December 2018

Dedications and Thanks:

Written with love and gratitude for all lovers, philosophers, peace warriors, and truth seekers from before and after me.

Special Appreciation and Love to
Jacob Nagro, Pamela Mackara, Alex Qualtire,
and Ben Trent (1988-2017).

Also, many thanks to all those who inspired and supported this book directly and indirectly, including and not limited to: 1000 Words, KGB, Gail Kent, Jay Nelson, Beau Tappan, Pippa, Stephen HaHa Hunt, Divina & Ray, Miguel Edwards, The McFaddens, Leo Torrez, Jaime Ivey, Robert Baca, Leif Hammond, Benny Capp, Bill Capp, John Helmer, Jonathan Spacer, John Poore, Scott Shepherd, Wayne Waltz, Joe and Susan, Brian, Kirk Loy, Ben Loy, Blu, Bo, Adam, Vida, Spirit, Rose, Dawnstarr, Aaron, Becca, Jan, Anne, Jenn, Monica, Rena, Christina, Maggie, Jessie, Terri, Mark Duggan, Scotty, Phil, Barry, Linda, Sherrisse, Nate, Kramer, all the Daves, and Cochise.

"One Heart", *2019*

Gabrielle Angel Dee Lilly

"These Are Dandelions"
~Angel Lilly, December 2018

Prologue:

There is a tiny spider I call "Grandmother". She lives somewhere near the center of my heart.

Grandmother probably isn't her real name, though she hasn't told me the story of her real name yet, so I still call her grandmother. She lives there, here, in my heart. For more than a thousand years she has lived here, weaving and spinning her threads. Lightness and dark. Silver and green. Warm kisses and silent snow blankets. She weaves them all into a tapestry of life-story.

She weaves tirelessly. She spins gold and silver threads into fantastic lifetimes. A little knot here. Another knot there. Day in and day out. Night after night after night. Year after year. Century after century. She dances out her webs of potentials, progresses, and productions. Always humming. Always with a loving spark in her shining spidery eyes. We sometimes call it play-ing. Sometimes we call it work. Sometimes we think it might all be a dream.

This is life; living alive.

Welcome.

Gabrielle Angel Dee Lilly

Truth. The pursuit of truth has been right up there with the pursuit of happiness, in the running for top pursuits of humankind, since at least as far back as our history goes. We wonder about it, wield it, and want it, for and from ourselves and one another.

There is evidence in cave paintings and in the first tales passed down around the fire in early societies, and in the first writings, of our pondering the truth of our consciousness. It seems we have long wondered about our place in the Universe, our place in society, our place in our own bodies. What are the rules? What should the laws be? Is this love true?

Centuries in, we continue to wonder. What is our individual purpose? How does my story fit into the fabric of societies story? We try on various roles. We adopt some of our favorite titles and labels. We become scientists, leaders, teachers, workers, lovers, parents, children. And still we wonder.

What is the real, relevant truth of everything, and of course, specific things? How do we fit in to the big picture? What does the big picture look like? Are we separate from nature somehow by way of our consciousness or imaginations? What happens when we die?

We often feel "out of place", or "born too late". We have accumulated countless stories about humankind's tumultuous relationship with our own truth of being. We also have countless stories of triumph, discovery, and delightful coming togethers of everything.

This book is a knot in my story. Perhaps it will be a useful thread in yours.

I 'tip my hat' here to my grandmother Dee, Socrates, Plato, Galileo, Aristotle, Sun Tzu, my mother, and every other person who has risked the soothing familiar to discover, uncover, and expand the unknown. I appreciate every person in history who, many times at the risk of their jobs, ego's stories, or at even the cost of freedom or life, have pursued this ever-winding path of the quest for truth. Including you; dear and courageous reader. You have made it this far. I think you must be quite brave.

Truth-seeking is not for the 'faint of heart'. It takes a strong heart to dive into the real questioning of truth, in all its simplicities, complexities and grand disillusionments. Do you have the courage to join us?

***

The picture I have in my mind to represent this book starts as a simple braid. Three strands. Or maybe it's a fish braid, with as many strands as we have. Each strand a bundle of strands. Human hair perhaps. Auburn, like mine. Like yours, lady, like yours. That's a Guinevere song reference. Hit the soundtrack.

I tied knots for years. I established patterns and then I broke them. It was a thing I did in the background of everything else. I still do that in different ways I suppose. This book is another exercise in making and breaking patterns.

This picture includes some colorful threads. Knots. Weaving. A tree. Wild horses. Foxtails. Bees and butterflies and wildflowers in a meadow. Honey, dripping when it's warm. It has hands in it, and some sensual things. An object made of clay. A crudely figured goddess. Something round. Maybe marbles. A heart-shaped stone.

Gabrielle Angel Dee Lilly

In the distance, out the window, there might be two people dancing in the moonlight. An owl maybe, in a tree. Probably a coyote, or a wolf, or a wild cat is keeping watch, just out of sight. I can see a feather lying in snow. Something soft and furry makes cute little animal noises from the shadows by the bushes. The air is crisp and cold and refreshing.

Somewhere out of sight, and yet still in this picture, there is an ocean. Rivers, mountains, and stones lie deep below the surface, in a cold lake.

At least one spider, darts off and onto pages. Her silver and gold threads glisten in the moonlight and in the sunlight. They are what will hold all of this together; firmly, lightly, strong. Delicate.

With perhaps just a little magic, this book will smell of cinnamon and cardamom and cloves right about here. Perhaps sweet baked apples and peppermint tea a bit later-on. Fresh bread. Toast. Lemon pie. Chai.

A hint of orange and vanilla and something a bit musky, like leather, might permeate every truth. I would love every page to take you to some good-smelling place. Every page is also potentially a different color, or two or three different colors. So subtly shifting, you might not have noticed they were colored at all, until now.

This story-meal tastes faintly of fried plantains and coconut and oatmeal cookies now and then. Cinnamon. In other parts it might remind you of arugula, pear and salmon salad. Slow simmering stew, or savory mushroom and spinach quiche.

Tomorrow is Christmas, and I am making sautéed kale with nuts and garlic and coconut. That is true.

Well, it was true when I wrote that part.

"Retrotrixct"
~GAL, 2019

Gabrielle Angel Dee Lilly

If this book were a Holiday card, the front would be a dragon with its tail wrapped around a window, looking into a traditional holiday season scene. Through the window, behind the pulled back curtains and around the spider webs, there would be a cheerful, green, holiday tree, decorated with all the animals. An owl. A coyote. A wolf. The raven. A bobcat. Housecats. Panther. Tiger. Snake. Heart. Guitar. Star. Spirals. Dragonfly. Pictures of people I love, including you and me. Two clocks. Three gifts.

On the table by the window, there would probably be a fishbowl with a whale in it, on a hand-woven or macramé table-cloth. Also, a heart shaped stone. A candle. A rubber band in the shape of a mobius strip. A shell. A few dragon scales. A peach. Apples. Glass marbles. A deck of cards. Jenga, maybe. Perhaps a colorful puzzle.

Near the table there might be a guitar. A sleeping house-cat and large dog would be curled up together, there, on a braided rug by the glowing, warm fire. It would feel like home on the best-feeling, most joyfully relaxing holiday that home ever imagined having.

You might notice a warm, unidentified pie, cooling on the window sill. A cartoony butterfly with an overstuffed bag, with two socks falling out of it, is flying by. She would be heading into our friendly neighborhood spider's web. Grandmother spider would be there too of course, spinning gold and silver yarns from her ass, hanging by a thread.

Behind the decorated tree, in a picture, or looking out another window, you might just make out what appears to be two people playing or dancing on a beach, near an ocean full of seashells and sea creatures. The sun is nearly setting.

Outside, in front of the window and the dragon, a yellow brick road would be winding. There might be a frog sitting off to one side, looking like it might hop across it. That is what frogs do, isn't it?

At the risk of ruining the 'end' I want to make clear from the start that I don't really believe in Truth, with a capital 'T". I am not sure about it anyhow. I have some theories about music and love, and chemistry and vibrations, and coherence and the connectedness of everything; but I am not certain what The One Real Truth is, if there ever is or was, or should be one. Mostly I think there probably shouldn't be just one, Ultimate Truth. To me, the Truth is just a crude summation of lots of tiny shiny specks of truth.

Perhaps the only real truth is change. Perhaps it is surface tension. Bi-directional spin. I often conclude the answer of every question to be "both", which is ultimately both: often not very useful; and nearly infinitely applicable to every dilemma.

Not long ago, I thought truth was closely related to honesty. In fact, I thought maybe truth and honesty were some of the most important things to me. My values. Come to find out, neither of those beliefs is really founded in truth. I have been lying to myself about honesty and truth all along. That's not really surprising though, I suppose, when I look at it with the handy-dandy story-making hack we call hindsight. There's more to being 'true' than truth and honesty, it turns out.

We still have authenticity. Don't we?

When I initially set out to actualize this book again, a little more than a year ago, I was hopeful I would settle into just a few Universal and Agreed upon truths which I would feel confident presenting to the world, in agreement with other philosophers who have come before me. And indeed, in many ways I suppose I have. It's "both", and "nothing". Even Forrest Gump figures that out by the end of the movie.

As I near the finish of authoring this book, I find myself swimming in truths. In certainty and uncertainty. Certainty about my uncertainty. Somewhere between the cliché lines and the hyperbole, there is a calm, quiet, soothing sense of truth growing in me. It's okay if it changes. In fact, it's probably always better if it sometimes does.

Everything is perfect in its imperfections.

"Be true to you."

Ultimately, at least for now, I believe that truth is relative. Under construct. Constant construction. Fluid. Like a river, really. Truth is whatever we make of it, and whatever we make it into. It is yours and it is mine. And not ours at all. It flows beyond time. Truth fluctuates and shifts with the seasons, and our perspectives, and what lights we are holding it up to. It is something of an enigma, truth. Sometimes useful and sometimes a wrecking ball for everything.

To my thinking and conclusions, truth is dependent on the proportion of perspectives, filters, lenses, purpose...so many things.

Obviously, this truth is not practically useful in many choice-making situations, though it does help me to not worry too much, about anything. Most of the time.

When I go out far enough in my time-space perspective, I find every truth falls apart. This is just one dimension of so many that we can imagine. Imagine how much there is that we can't imagine!

Not too long though. I don't want you to get lost out in the vast and ever-expanding outer space of infinity just yet.

Come back inside. Let's get closer.

I also feel I should point out, I believe in what might seem like 'conflicting truths'. I can hold seemingly opposing ideas in a realm of possible truths at the same time. "Both" can be true. And, neither. At the same time.

By practicing this idea of holding two or more, sometimes seemingly conflicting ideas as possible truth at the same time, we can more effectively communicate with each other. Even when we have very different beliefs, we can find common ground.

I believe this is a good skill for us all to cultivate more of as we move into a more global social arena. As we expand our connections, we will benefit from learning to resolve conflicts and differences of perspective peacefully. That's my opinion.

We can agree to hold each other and our differences in a kinder frame of mind, and maybe even a loving space. Especially when we do not understand each other. Attitude is everything. Or was that intension? Vibration? Juxtaposition?

"It's all about the relative perspective and proportionality of one thing to another."

I believe it is important to examine what we believe from time to time, especially in times of change, disruption, or dissatisfaction. It's important for us to have working truths and commonly accepted truths.

I also think it is crucial for many of us to be questing for Universal truth, much of the time. To me, this is the Great Mystery, which ultimately propagates life. It's as close to a god as I can get behind, right now.

Over time, we can learn to see things in a different way. We can expand our horizons and add more depth of field to our view. We can cultivate more effective communication across cultures and languages. When I think of all the many beautiful languages we have developed so far, and of the times and places we have yet to get to, I get excited about the future. Do you?

The mystery moves us forward. Life is constantly discovering itself. Creating itself. Recovering and rediscovering itself. It just goes on and on, my friend. Just like that one song that never ends. Each iteration a slight potential for variation. This is evolution.

The intention of this book is not to get you to agree with me about what the truth is. It is more of a reflection on what my own experiences have taught me about truth so far. This is an exploration of my own story and of my own beliefs.

Mostly, I hope this is an invitation to you. I hope you will examine what truth is to you, a little more often. I hope you will be inspired to be more 'true to you', whatever that means to you. And, I hope you might lighten up a little bit, smile, and consider that there might be more than one truth at any given time. No one needs to be right. No one needs to be wrong.

We need each other to be mostly happy and whole and able to let things go; in the future I am imagining. We can build amazing scenes and experience fantastic rides. We just might need to release some of the old beliefs which are cluttering up the way. Loosen up our grip on being right and someone else being wrong. I hope you will "give yourself permission to imagine a better future and make it come true" (Imagine it Forward, 2018).

Give truth a little more space to breath, if you will. Air it out now and then and let go of made-up beliefs which might have served you well at some point in time and are now just clutter, getting in your way. Maybe getting in our way.

Consider that you don't need to be wrong in order for someone else to be right and have a different truth, or a difference of opinion. Get rid of 'old and busted'. Make room for the 'New Hotness' (Men in Black II).

What is true for you today?

I hope this book will make a thought-provoking read from cover to cover; and also at any random page, or even part of any page. I think it should work well as a functioning tool for any light-hearted lightening work, or even as an effective change agent all on its own, if one would like to pick it up; open it; and soak in just a little of my cosmic comedic wisdom.

You can also try just holding the book, or even thinking about it from afar, though I am not sure what effect, if any, that will have.

Please tell me if you find out.

This is not a love song, nor am I posing any serious theory about truth here, really. And, although I AM interested in the questions of observations as a vehicle of scientific evidence and prediction theory, (*Pursuit of Truth by W. V. Quine), this is not a discussion of atomic facts vs whatever the opposite of those are. This is just that. A story about stories.

This is more of a stroll through the spools of colorful threads and yarns in my mind. It's a quick dip in my personal current pools of truth, and a playful tribute to all the other truth-seekers who have come before me. It's also some kind of love-letter to those lovers of life, liberty, truth, and happiness who come after me.

So, welcome. Take off your coat and shoes. Squeeze my hand. Take a deep breath, and then, let it out.

All the way now. Let's go.

***

Push your toes into the soft grassy earth. Look at all those bright yellow dandelions. Is that a spider? Climb a few streamside trails with me. Let's dance and play with what I find to be true right now, in my mind.

"The seed of everything is in everything else."
~Anaxagoras (c. 500-428 BCE)

The Rules:

Rule #1: Keep Calm.

Rule #2: Relax.

Rule #3: Enjoy!

The Call:

Riiiiing. Riiiiing.
Hello?
Hi, Henry? Herbert? Helga? Heidi? Dancer? Prancer?
…
Yes?
Your ride is waiting outside for you.
Will you join me for the heart-web tour of possibility?
…
Be right there.

Click.

"A Horse In My Window"
~Angel Lilly, January 2019

The Ride

Contents

"Coyotrix"
~Angel Lilly, January 2019

Your Map:

The basic format of this book is

1. I will start us off with a swimming foundation, drenched in playful sensory stimulation with a hint of uncertainty. Next, I will bang on pots and pans and strum my guitar on the porch of your resistance, hoping you will let me in eventually. I might be kidding. I suppose we will have to wait and see.

2. Next, I will attempt to stack and weave 47 short 'chapters, or stories; made up 'on the fly' explorations of catch phrases and possible or 'posed' truths. If I am successful, this might remind you of macramé or beadwork or one of those spiraling braided rugs made from old worn out t-shirts.

3. To maximize the potential positive effects of this book, each exploration ends with some space where I encourage you to jot down any of your own notes, doodles, or coffee stains you feel like adding. I might get some of my artwork in before the first edition publishing. We will see.

4. The Epic Epilogue was originally the Introspective Introduction. It is where I explain why I wrote this book. I have added several experimental and playful sections to the back of the book. I invite you check them out if you feel like it.

5. Your personal invitation to explore your own truths, and my contact info in case you want to contact me, are also in the back, and throughout.

6. The suggested reading list is kinda dope. Check it out.

7. Don't forget to play every day. #PlayEveryDay

"Over the Mountain"
~Angel Lilly, January 2019

Gabrielle Angel Dee Lilly

The Keys:

My desires for this book are to spark your imagination and your smile; warm and open your heart, and to encourage you to be brave and light hearted enough to dive into your own beliefs a bit. I aim to forge connections between past and present truths, and weave together threads of my own personal truths into the perpetual fabric of everything.

I invite you to put down, or at least sheath your weapons of presumption and resentments. Take off your armor and play with me a while. What have you got to lose, other than perhaps a few old, outdated beliefs and stories that are no longer serving you?

I invite you to join me and contribute to the movement I see trending towards peaceful global domination with freewill, communication, coherence, and kindness. I join forces with a growing army of peace warriors and empowerment leaders, and greatness window openers. Dr. Joe Dispenza, Peter Diamandis, Tom Bilyeu, Jason Silva, Kyle Cease, Lewis Howes, Gary Vaynerchuck, Evan Carmichael, Marissa Peers, JP Sears, Rob Dyrdic, Naveen Jain, Jay Samit, Layla Martin, Anna Akana, Lily Singh, Oprah, and Jay Shetty come to mind at this time. The list of influencers and contributors is extensive and impressive, and growing every day. When will you join us?

"My warm pink stone heart"
~Angel Lilly, January 2019

Gabrielle Angel Dee Lilly

"Three Truths"
~Angel Lilly, January 2019

Here are three truths you should know about this book:

1.You can read it cover-to-cover or open it to any page and read any amount of it you like. Of course you can. You can do that with any book you like. This one is made for that. It is linear and non-linear. It circles.

The feelings, the fragrance, the colors, the textures, and the truth, should seep into you from any contact...maybe even from a distance. Like anything, it does have a cumulative effect, however. Proximity, dosage and timing matter. The order matters, and it doesn't matter. The whole thing works together even better than any single tiny shiny speck, or chapter, of it does; even though they all do work perfectly on their own, on a good day.

2.We are making this up. I am making this up now, and you are making this up later. Grandmother spider made it all up already a lot of times, some time ago. How everything tastes to you, isn't only up to you. There are a lot of ins and out to it. A lot of tasty subplots and subtle morsels.

We get to choose. We get to decide what and how we experience this. The choice isn't always obvious or easy. That is what makes it interesting. Move along now.

3.I have laid down some somewhat loose, swimming foundations. Not the sort I would recommend building on, on their own. To build on any of this, we will need to share perspectives and grow our truths. Nurture them side by side. Weave them together into something fantastic and strong, and flexible.

Gabrielle Angel Dee Lilly

The truth requires you to add your own perspectives, your own heart, your own truths. Your choices matter. Your perspectives matter. You matter.

I hope you will feel more secure and open-minded about your own beliefs after you finish this book. Or maybe I want to rock your belief-boat a little bit. That depends on what you believe is true, I imagine.

If you feel firm enough to bounce a message back to me through the ether somehow and share your perspective with me in some way, please do. I will be extra thrilled if I hear from you. Writing this book has been its own thrilling reward, however, in and of itself. I highly recommend writing a book about your own truths, by the way. It really does help put everything in perspective.

If any of this offends you, and I am guessing some of it might, you are of course, free to do whatever you like with that feeling. I do hope you will believe and remember that my intentions are not to offend anyone whatsoever, and so any success at doing so is purely accidental, if not fortuitous. Most likely it's a good thing because that means I've got you thinking about what you believe, and maybe why. You can take it however you want to though, of course.

If I offend you in any way, although that is not my intention, I'd like to say in advance, you are welcome.

***

I read a short story about a dog recently, which went something like this: Imagine you see a dog tied to a tree and you bend down to say hello. The dog snarls at you angrily, so you back away, thinking to yourself, *'Geez! That's a really mean dog. I better leave it alone.'*

Just then you notice that the dog's leg is stuck in a trap. It's leg is cut, broken, and bleeding. Now you recognize the fear and pain in the dog's eyes. It snarls at you even more. You feel differently about the dog now that you see it is vulnerable. You have to make a choice about the role you will play. You get to decide if you will be the hero, the victim, the passerby. You get to tell the story of how it was too dangerous to try to help, or you can try to do something. Whatever you do is really up to you and for you. The story will go on however it goes.

I try to remember this story whenever I am feeling trapped or angry, or whenever anyone seems like they are being unduly mean or insensitive to me. For so many different reasons, we all feel trapped sometimes. We all go through things that make us bleed. We all have wounds to feed.

What I would love you to see, when you look through me, is a richly colored, deliciously fragrant tapestry of infinite blissful discovery, sweet darkness balanced delightfully with gold and silver light, threads of every feeling dancing in moonbeams.

"What color is this to you?"

Start your engines.

"If you don't have a vision of the future, then you are living in the past, and you will never arrive at that future. Feelings and emotions are the results of past experiences. A majority of people spend their lives talking about the past reasons they will not arrive at the future they want."
~~Dr. Joe Dispenza, You Are the Placebo, 2018

"ODeeOne"
~Angel Lilly, January 2019

truth one

"There is only one Truth."

That is the Truth of Here and Now. The Truth of You, according to you. The present. Just this moment exists in space-time. Even that is probably, at least mostly, if not all, a grand, or perhaps a not-so-grand, illusion. It could actually be a tiny illusion, blown vastly out of proportion. You never can tell what your perceptions are lying about for certain, can you?

In any case, what you consider the truth now, is probably mostly made up. Fabricated fabrications. Old tattered stories and worn out memories piled up to amount to present perceptions. Everything else is an increasingly distant memory or imagination of an illusion. Twice removed from any 'real truth', at best. A distant cousin, really. Hardly even worth inviting to the truth family table on holidays.

Might as well get into it then.

So here it is. All of it. The truth; as it is for me, just now. Not the "Truth", mind you, with a capital "T", as that isn't up to only me. The truth. Lower case 't'. It's yours to make whatever you will of it. And I of mine.

There is only one truth, and we all know the truth. It lives through and in each of us. Of course, we will change the words of it. We will change the design from time to time. We might see some of it the same way and want to put it in a box of truths we agree on, and call those, 'Agreed Upon Truths'. If enough of us agree on some of them for a very long time, or they serve our hopes and dreams and desires very well, we can call them 'Universal Truths', or maybe even "Laws".

If we are able to predict them reliably, and they seem to hold true without needing us to believe them, then we usually call them 'Scientific Facts', at least recently. They are all still just working truths to me. Stories, in a context of assumptions. To my thinking, when I go all the way down the rabbit-hole of self-reflection and my own perception of truth -- all the way down it -- and come out the other side, it's all relative.
It all comes down to enjoying the ride. Enjoy right now.

Savor the flavors.

Any thought in your head, anything that takes you out of the present moment, is your ego-story. It can be a beautiful story, and I hope it is. It is still just a made-up story. The beauty of that is, we can change what we don't like.

The rub of it is, the ego does not know the difference between dying and growing. So our egos resist change. Often quite melodramatically. It usually takes either some great inspiration or some great trauma or tragedy to overcome our own resistance and transform. Appreciate the transformation. This is what we are here for.

Everything is dependent on the systems we put it through and into. Data is dependent on its collectors, its processors, its underlying beliefs. Ours, I mean; since we are the meat machines which, as far as we give credit so far, are the main ones who care to find out.

I am not sure why we think we are the only ones evolving into self-awareness. It seems like every speck of life has Some capacity, drive, and opportunity to experience evolution, growth, expansion and collapse. That's what this cycle seems to be all about from here, to me. Of course, I can only see things through my own reflection, in a sense, so it makes sense that I compare all experiences of existence to my own.

Anyhow, I feel I need to lay it out in front, that I don't really believe in some Ultimate Great Truth, with a capital "T", unless we call it "The Great Mystery", and then I can get on board. That's really just semantics though isn't it? Maybe we can agree on the feeling of some things, even when the words try to get in the way.

I do believe in dragons, or at least an energy of vast potential outside time and space which I like to call dragon energy. I think current science is calling that, "the quantum field". I have also embodied the energy of Santa Claus, the tooth-fairy, a housemaid, and the Easter bunny, among others. So, do with that whatever you will.

I believe in infinite potential and the possibility of what seems improbable. I believe in love. I believe in the power of music. I believe in things I can't see, and even in things not any of us have yet dreamed.

Now that I have finished laying this swimming foundation in deep, deep water, let's dive to it, shall we?

Seize the day.

Vroom. Vroom.

"Do not love leisure. Waste not a minute. Be bold. Realize the Truth, here and now!"
~Swami Sivananda

Gabrielle Angel Dee Lilly

"Fish Eye Kiss"
~Angel Lilly, January 2019

truth two

"It's all made up."

This follows nicely from the first truth, since it gives you any amount of liberty you want to pick up and carry around. You can design whatever belief system best serves the outcomes you desire.

I made that sound simple, when, really though, it can be quite tricky. A bit sneaky even. Because we tend to keep things from ourselves. We deceive ourselves and put things endlessly in our own way. And then we make up really awful stories about how it is everyone else's fault. So, the bullshit can get quite thick. "I'm Kidding!" That's a Gilbert Gottfried reference. I'm not really kidding though.

Gabrielle Angel Dee Lilly

It's simpler than all that. Really what I mean is, it's the totality of everything making itself and everything else up at the same time. It's all of us. And not just us, it's 'them' too.

Of course, as I see it, we are really them and they are actually us, in the end. The whole thing loops around quite nicely to show me that ultimately, I am just responsible for my own perceptions, my own choices, my own responses. Just like you are responsible for yours. If I don't like what I am getting, it's really nobody's fault but mine.

I can change. You can change. We will change. And some things will stay the same.

You are what you eat. And read. And put on your feet. And put your hands into. You are what you believe. You are what you love, and the stories you tell yourself about what loves you.

Be mindful of what you digest, touch, love, say, and do, for it becomes you.

We all get a pre-programed response choice box, and pockets full of freewill and adventurous imaginations. Then we get to build on those. Add new responses. Take out the old outdated ones. Exercise our freewill and adventurous imaginations so they are ready to take us on a wild and fun ride anytime, day or night. It's a beautiful, amazing thing, this life.

Truly.

It's all made up, but you are not the only one making all this stuff up. More is going on than you think. There's a lot more that you don't know, than you do know. And, there is a lot more that you don't know you don't know, than you do know you don't know. That is hard to write and say, even though it hardly has any words in it.

While we are on the subject of religion, let's just get this out of the way again: I don't know what happens after this life. I don't know if there is a god or goddess or afterlife or any kind of judgement outside this life. I am not purposing we adopt any new theories or get rid of any specific old ones. Not here anyway. Not now.

I do know that acting as if there is something after this life, often gives a decent guide for designing a pretty decent life. "Why not tell yourself a nice fairy tale if it makes living more pleasant?" (Alan Akrin).

For sure, there is a lot more going on than you think, or that you can possibly be aware of. A lot more than you even have the tools or equipment or apparatii to perceive or imagine perceiving. As far as I can tell, it doesn't help to take any of it too seriously, or personally. Life is much too important to take it seriously. Lighten up.

So, are you ready? Deep breathe now. In, and then let go. Shoulders rolled back and down. Spine in a line. Relax. Sit up a little and lean back. Put your ears over your shoulders. Tuck your chin, and your tail bone. Breathe out. Lighten up. "This will only hurt for a second." (Hunter T. Thompson).

Was that too soon?

Gaze softly in the direction you think my words are pointing. Laugh with me. Let true meaning find itself in you. I invite you to find your own truth where we agree and disagree, equally. Find it and hold it loosely.

...lightly now...

The good news is, there's really no 'wrong way', other than what feels wrong to you. When you are in a good mood, in a high vibrational state, really in love, everything works. Anything can work.

Get Happy. Get jiggy with it. Giggity. Let go of whatever is in your way. Don't stop and fight it. Don't kick it till it hurts. Just reach for what you want. Look into the eyes of who you love. Leave the rest to the rest.

You might think this sounds lazy. You might worry that your family, the world, the Universe might fall apart without you worrying and struggling and suffering about it. Don't worry. You will find plenty of work to do, and it will add up to a much more positive difference when you align with your true, playful, joyful, self, first. Try it, you might like it.

If you find yourself thinking 'I can't. I won't. I shouldn't. Poor me. This always happens. I knew this was going to happen. This is why I might as well go eat worms.' Instead of moaning about everything that displeases you. Try asking yourself more questions?

Why do I think that? How is this serving me? What do I really want to feel? What do I need to become? Is this helping? What can I do to help? How can I communicate more effectively? What is trying to emerge?

Would you choose this right now? Are you keeping something in your life just because it has been there a long time? Are the things you want, really the things you want, or are they the things you think you should want, because you think other people want them?

Instead of telling the same old story of how you can't, you shouldn't, or you should; tell me a story of what you can become. Tell me what you want. Tell me what you are grateful for, and what you appreciate about it. Tell me what you are looking forward to. Tell me how you are getting ready, and what you are getting for.

We can have both.

"Smile, smile, smile at your mind as often as possible. Your smiling will considerably reduce your mind's tearing tension."
~Sri Chinmoy

Gabrielle Angel Dee Lilly

"Unicorns' Keep"
~Angel Lilly, January 2019

truth three

"Be Kind"

*Skip this chapter if you hate the word Fuck, or f-words.

"You don't have to be nice or kind to live a good life, but it fucking helps." ~ Gabrielle Angel-Hey-That's-Me-Lilly

Be nice. This one was not originally number three. I debated, and still might, frankly, move it back further so 'the f bomb', as the nuns are calling it these days, won't hit so quickly, right up front.

"One good thing about music, when it hits you, you feel okay" (Bob Marley, Trench Town Rock).

Is that really true? Can you imagine a bunch of nuns talking and any of them using that phrase, "f-bomb"? I guess I can, I just did...and now, so can you.

You're welcome.

Anyhow, I decided to put it right up front near the start to get us off on firm footing as to the kind of person I really am. Did I not do this already, earlier?

This should give you plenty of time to cleanse your soul, repent, and still make it to heaven by the time this life is over, if that is what you decide you should do after reading this book. Meanwhile, I release myself of any burden of self-restraint when it comes to using my authentic voice in whatever language I feel like using; right here, right now. Not that I was feeling any particular restraint up to this point.

I also want to mention, about here, how it is a brilliant demonstration of its own validity as a point, because the word 'fucking' causes just a little rub. It's at least vaguely abrasive, even to me, and I fucking love it. Not the act of, most of the time. The word, I mean. Fuck. Like I love crunchy peanut butter, sort of. That's an inside aside, which just refers to the way some of us like our peanut butter crunchy and some like it smooth.

Even though, crunchy is clearly better.

This quote demonstrates both aspects of its own truth. You don't have to be kind or nice. I sometimes choose not to be. And it does fucking help. To be nice, that is.

Some of you probably wish I hadn't used so many f-bombs already, and maybe you would prefer I stop before you find it so abrasive you can't hear me over the distraction of all that scratching. I can promise there will be fewer f-bombs from here on out.

We all benefit when we are kind and nice to each other. We all suffer more when one of us decides to be an asshole because some-other-one of us was an asshole. Asshole for asshole just stinks up the whole place.

What I really want to get across is, that being nice--not the fake kind of nice, mind you--genuinely caring about others, and trying to help them feel good, is good for you and everyone around you. It helps your heart.

Your heartbeat actually gets smoother, steadier, and more coherent when you are nice. A smoother, steadier heart makes you healthier, happier, and more able to make good decisions for yourself and those you love (Dr. Joe Dispenza, 2018). Your face and your vibration will be more attractive to other happy people too. That's not just my opinion.

Being kinder to others can actually help you love them and yourself more. Others will most likely feel compelled to like you more too. It's called reciprocity. Humans are seemingly compelled to exchange things for other things, favors for favors, eyes for eyes. Love for love…

My grandmother Dee's version of this was "you get more flies with honey than with vinegar." I don't actually know if this is true, or why you would want to get very many flies...and now I am thinking more about it, I think it depends on the types of honey and vinegar and flies...probably temperature has something to do with it. I guess that might be the fake nice I was thinking of earlier.

The point is, being nice is easier, and makes things easier for others, generally. So generally, you should fucking try to be nice. You already know this is true.

Gabrielle Angel Dee Lilly

For you freaky f-word fans: Frequently, Fridha felt faintly fickle, for Frank fortuitously failed French Fiesta Fridays. Free flying frogs? I have a couple stories I could tell you about frogs. Another time, perhaps. Forward!

"Winter Desert Flowers"
~Angel Lilly, December 2018

Gabrielle Angel Dee Lilly

"StarMeadowCorn"
~Angel Lilly, January 2019

"The truth will set you free,
but first it will piss you off!"
~Gloria Steinem

the fourth truth

"Clichés happen for a reason."

Is that true? It might be. There is usually a lot of truth in a cliché, and some untruth. I love clichés, because to me they are like standing dares to use them in ways that add to or subtract from their agreed upon meanings or validity. Markers of our linguistic evolution.

It's important to examine them in our current time and space though, and not just accept them because they have been repeated so many times. They sound familiar so we give them extra credit. We should give them an extra shrewd eye. A shrew eye?

"Only boring people get bored." was another of my grandmother's favorite sayings, which was passed down to my mother and then to me. Dorothy Ritzhaupt Lilly, my mother's mom. She was what people call 'a character'. And an alcoholic. Most people were back then. Maybe we still are.

Gabrielle Angel Dee Lilly

Dorothy married my grandfather, James Alexander Lilly Sr. She was his first wife of three. She was my grandma Dee. Until recently, I told myself a story about how she named me, and I was named after her. Gabrielle Dee. Last week, in a casual conversation with my mother, I learned that it was actually my step-grandmother, Martha, my grandfather's second wife, who gave me the name Gabrielle.

My mother wanted to name me Galadriel. That part of the story has remained the same. She would still like to call me GiGi for short. She calls me Gabs or Gabby though. Gabrielle sometimes. Not Angel. I call her by her first name, not mom or mother. I suppose that is just another clue that I might be a bit strange. Funny, isn't it, what is in a name? We put a lot of weight on our names.

So, my grandmother Dee did not name me. This changes nothing. I admire her greatly still, though she died when I was ten or eleven. It's entertaining to think about how the stories we tell about ourselves form our identities, and how then we become slaves to our own egos, the very same made up stories. Especially when you factor in how often we don't even like ourselves. Whatever the arbitrary details of your life and name are, I hope you love who you are in your own story. If you don't, well, it's never too late to change the way you look at things.

It's up to you to make yourself. If you don't like the story of your life, change it. Make yourself whatever you want to be. What else are you going to do before you die?

It's up to you to make your life interesting. To be, and to keep becoming, interesting, and interested. It's no one else's job to do that for you. And again, I feel compelled to mention, there is such a vast shit-ton of stuff a person can do. It just isn't possible to be bored unless you are choosing not to do anything, which is fine and even can be healthy from time to time.

Just save the drama for something more worthy of whine. Stop complaining about it. If you do decide to whine, get some cheese and crackers too; and make an event, or a night of it. Get it out of your system and then move.the.fuck.on.

If you want to do nothing, embrace doing nothing! Savor the flavor of it. Sit and stare into space. Count dots on the ceiling. Netflix and chill. Imagine yourself in infinite space with wind you can only see but not feel or hear waving through your hair. If you ever hear yourself saying those absurd words, "I'm bored." Please stop. Remember this moment and for the love of all that is right and true, do something. Anything. There is just so much you can do. Even if it's nothing. Do it on purpose when you think of it.

Ever rolled down a grassy hill? Tried walking around the block with your eyes closed? Tossed and caught a rubber ball as many times as possible without dropping it while walking, starting your count over when you drop it and seeing how you can beat your old best, almost every.single.time? Blow your own freaking mind? Kick rocks? You get the idea.

Do something or enjoy doing nothing. Don't waste the space in my mental earholes with words that add up to you complaining about having nothing to do. That is literally one of the most absurd things people say.

Gabrielle Angel Dee Lilly

Like, totes.

That reminds me of another popular phrase. "Two wrongs don't make a right." Simple math, really. Two negatives add up to more negative, just like two positives add up to more positive. The sum of all our choices adds up to the overall experience we coexist in.

Vibrationally, we are nearly all wired similarly, in my experience. It doesn't even have to be applied to any 'grand scheme or plan' and you don't need to consider anyone else, though if you do, it still holds well true. What is good for the whole is what is good for you, which is in turn, what is good for the whole. In small circles and broad, it helps to be kind. Do your best to do what you feel is right, and travel light.

Dragging your own vibration down to meet someone else you feel is wrong is the quickest way to become what you say you hate. When you recognize what you consider wrong, if you can, be grateful for it. Appreciate that you recognized it. Take the opportunity to choose what you consider right. This is living by deliberate design. This is living a good life!

You get to choose what is good for you, and you get to choose to choose what is right, when you want to. Choosing to do what you say you think is wrong because someone else is choosing to do what you think is wrong, is right up there on the top shelf of absurd things people do.

Whatever you decide to become, I am certain you can do better than becoming what you hate.

Now, get out there and get some love on ya!

"You can't get blood out of a turnip."
~American Proverb

"Everyone wants the truth
but no one wants to be honest."
~Anonymous

Gabrielle Angel Dee Lilly

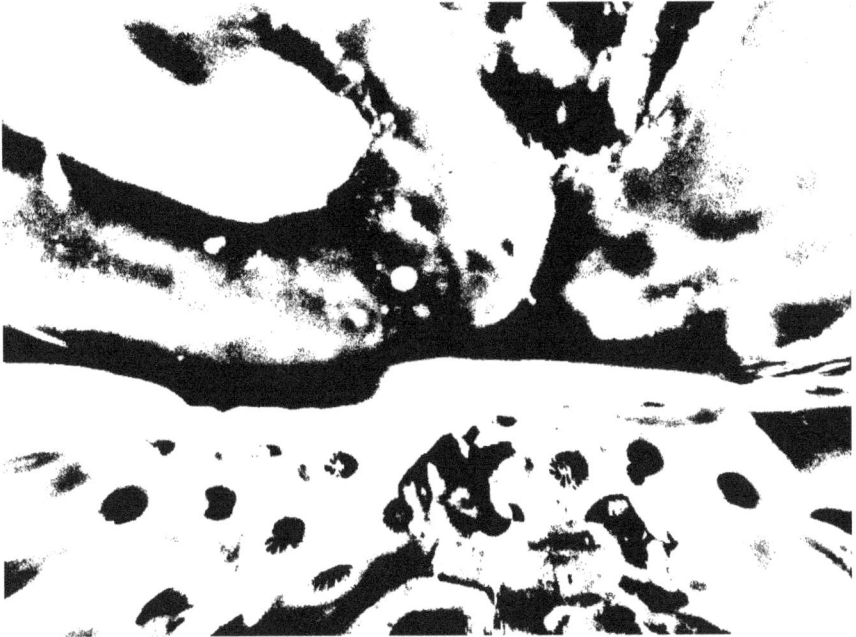

"Potentialscape"
~Angel Lilly, January 2019

truth five

"Your body is a magnificent meat machine!"

Your body is the only thing you can't live without. You might think you can't live without water or food or love or hugs. Really, what you mean when you say, "can't live", is that you might lose your residency in this body. Your body is the only thing that is going to be with you for this entire journey. Give it a little love! Give it some of your time and attention every day. You probably won't be sorry if you do. You might be sorry if you don't.

Having a healthy and able body is one of the biggest factors for determining if you will succeed in designing and building a life you enjoy, or, enjoying any life, whoever designs and builds it. Fact is, a fit body is going to get you more places, more money, more mating and all other choices, and most likely more time alive.

It feels good to be fit. Fit, ideally is strong and flexible, supple, relaxed, calm, capable of action.
Fit isn't the key to happiness, or a guarantee you will be happy though. Happiness, or rather, satisfaction and purpose, that is something potentially more elusive than fitness, and just as simple to achieve.

I know what it feels like to be at war with the body you live in. I was diagnosed with chronic and incurable inflammatory autoimmune disorders before I was ten. I got hives nearly every night; sometimes mild, sometimes debilitating, for about twelve years. Chronic urticaria. Brain fog. Rheumatoid arthritis. Psoriasis. Welts. Rashes. Anxiety. Anger. Lots of pills. Spots. Dizzy spells. Doctors. Nurses. More pills. Toss in a couple traumatic brain injuries and sprinkle lightly with mild sexual harassment and severe bullying. Par for the course; growing up in the country and being 'different' in a small town. Somehow I still managed nearly straight A's and to skip a couple grades.

Much of my early teen years I lived in fear of losing my prescription medicine or waking up with my throat swelling shut, or my face deformed from blotchy burning welts. I took a zero in PE every day because I was ashamed to undress in front of the other girls. I was so self-conscious I couldn't pee in a public restroom if anyone else was in there.

Gabrielle Angel Dee Lilly

It wasn't the best way to go through puberty. In hindsight, I probably should have tried harder to avoid it. Looking back, it's also little wonder I started drinking and cutting myself for attention at age 12 and was a pretty 'full-blown' text-book alcoholic by age 14. I think most people were. Maybe they still are.

Later, in my 30's, I got fibroids, cysts, and Hashimoto's thyroiditis. Again, par for the course. You get what you get ready for. I stopped going to doctors after that for the most part. I currently live with relatively mild and occasional symptoms of pancreatitis, colitis, arthritis, brain fog, numbness and some neurological disfunction. I manage it with healthy eating, positive mindset, moving meditations, hydrotherapy, bouncing, snowboarding, singing, and breathing. It's pretty much just like getting older.

You just do the best you can with what you've got, from where you're at.

Twice in this body, I have gained over 100 pounds of excess body fat. I weighed over 250 pounds in my twenties. I worked hard to lose the weight. I changed my lifestyle, and my attitude. I got into dancing and martial arts again, lost most of it, and was in pretty amazing shape. Then slowly, or maybe it was quickly, over a few years, I ballooned back over 250 pounds again in my thirties. I was depressed. Sick. In pain. And relatively happy in some ways. I had friends. I kept up on my bills. I grew my business and cruised through school.

Twice I have slowly regained control of my body and returned to a higher level of fitness after realizing my relationship with my body had turned toxic. I have learned and relearned to love and communicate with myself enough to regain hope and a functional level of fitness and relative happiness after slipping slowly down the slope of not caring enough, or not feeling worthy enough of my own care. And I still had plenty of happiness while I was fat.

The point is, I understand that it is one thing to SAY you should love your body and be good to yourself, and it is another to learn how to do it over a lifetime. To live a healthy, well-rounded, fulfilling life. You've got to put in the time, like with any relationship. Learn to communicate with your own body. Listen. Set boundaries. Articulate your desires. Forgive. Give yourself time. Train your body and your brain. When you find yourself failing, begin again. Start over. Again, and again.

I know it is worth it. YOU are worth it. I am worth it. Every body is worth it. Even if you think you got a raw deal and your body seems to be less fully-functional than most others, I assure you, it is still freaking amazing! Being born a human, right here, right now, does seem like quite a lucky draw.

As I approach age 50, I feel healthier and more capable than ever. It's all about how you live. I think anyone who has done any healing will agree that healing is an ongoing affair, not just a one-time gig. A significant part of this process, for me, has been learning to integrate the body with the mind, and to train my brain out of telling such shitty stories so much of the time.

We have clusters of neurons to process and interface in the gut, brain, and heart. I call that the mind. Our brains are like hardware, interfacing with the body, and our minds are like software, interfacing with the entire Universe. The brain can train the body, the mind can train the brain. Every cell in the body, and perhaps outside the body, is part of the mind.

There is increasing evidence our bodies can communicate with other bodies, outside ourselves, through the mind. I suspect it may be in continual communication with every other speck of this Universe, to some degree. Perhaps we owe it to ourselves then, and in some way to the entire Universe, to be the highest version of selves that we can achieve.

The brain is a fantastic imagination machine, and processing tool, that lives in a dark boney wrinkled up box of bone we call "skull". It spends all its awake time solving problems and thinking up terrible stories and making chemical cocktails to reinforce its own illusions of reality. It is best to keep a brain in check. Give it important things to do.

"Nothing will work unless you do."
~Maya Angelou

"Tyrannescape"
~Angel Lilly, January 2019

truth number six

"Failure is not just an option; it's a necessity."

Failure is part of the path to success. I also love to say, *"Anything worth doing well, is worth doing wrong."* We like to share our successes, our benchmarks, our masterpieces, and tend not only to withhold credit to the failures necessary along the way, we often vilify failure, as if it was the counterweight to success. We act as if failure will somehow crush us, make us smaller; and so it does.

We put tired piles, and thorny, shame-filled crumbs of failure in our own way nearly anytime we start to feel light enough to fly. Possibilities and improvements be damned! We make failure so heavy that the weight of it crushes itself. Our failures and near misses crush our own sense of self or even our mission sometimes. We let the weight of failure bury our ambitions, when instead we should be stepping onto the familiar and sturdy back of our failures. Failure is where you can find firm footing for your future. Step up.

I don't mean try to fail, or that you should be content to fail all the time, or that you should feel like your failures make YOU a failure. It's all a work in progress. Part of the process. Just don't be afraid to fail. Understand that it will happen, and when it does, cheerfully look for what you can learn from it, and move on.

Our failures, like our scars, are what make us uniquely beautiful! This is where we came from, how far we've come, what we learned from, what we discovered, what surprises us, what leads us to new theories, new insights, new questions, and new connections.

The best engineers will tell you they plan to find new ways of failing regularly, in order to explore, to gain new insights, to test and see. Check out Impact Theory on YouTube for an ever-expanding library of examples of people using their failures as stepping stones to success. To find out what happens that is predictable, and what happens that surprises you, you have to be willing to risk failure sometimes.

We need to have a willingness to not know in order to try new things. We would do well to be okay being unsure, even willing to try in the face of absolutely certain failure, in the pursuit of truth.

This might be the truth I am most passionate about. I recently learned that my dominant archetype, according to numerology, is the Outlaw or Rebel. This oracle resonated with me pretty well, though I also refuse to be 'pigeon holed' or pinned down to a single archetype to 'dominate' my lifestyle. I don't like being locked in a box. Like any cat, I love to climb in on my own and sit for a while though.

I relate very much to most of the archetypes, and I bet most people relate to at least one or two. How about you?

All that said, it's important to approach and move through failures with a positive attitude. As positive as you can muster. The more positive you can be, the better outcomes you will see. Use positive words. Think positive thoughts. Train yourself in that direction and your life will continue to get better.

Don't ever think of yourself as a loser. Learn when you lose. Be a lifelong learner. Learn when you win. When you make discovery, expanding your awareness and understanding, and developing skills your goals, then 'failures' are universally excellent opportunities to grow, learn, and expand.

If you catch your brain putting you down for not getting it right the first time, just snap out of it. Turn that train of thought around and remember that you are in this for 'the long haul'. Flip the switch. Find the lesson. Move on.

Don't hang on to a mistake just because you spent a long time making it.

It doesn't mean it was a waste of time if you let something go. It just means you are finished with that part of your story. You learned the lesson. Let go. Make room for something new. Let go of old beliefs and make room for new ways of understanding, new ways of being, new ways of loving.

Ask more questions!

"The truth is more important than the facts."
~Frank Lloyd Wright

"The Big Night Why"
~Angel Lilly, January 2019

Gabrielle Angel Dee Lilly

the truth about sevens

"The Great Mystery"

"Mystery ist gut." It's okay to not know the truth. Let's hope we never figure everything out. I am pretty sure that would be the saddest end to everything I can imagine.

'And then, one day, every speck of being knew everything. Every story. Every perspective. Every future, past, present event. All the inner workings and connections, how it all fit together just like a simple cake, how it all got put together, woven there by a tiny spider in the center of a very large heart.'

Imagine all the mystery was one day gone. Worse than the music dying. This would mean the death of all being, all living, all quest, all hero, all romance, all tragedy, all comedy, every delightful dramatic surprise. All of it would end. We would just be a giant story about nothing. The cold, vast, nothing next to nothing next to nothing. That's from an ATW Song, "Internet", cue the soundtrack (All Them Witches, Internet, Sleeping Through the War, 2018).

Even then, if we survived, we would sail into infinity, wondering, hoping, searching, for something unknown. Something to figure out. Something new to reveal itself. Some problem to solve. Perhaps we could find some residual debts left behind somewhere to pay. Some sense of purpose.

Then we might get bored.

So be happy with the mysteries you have. Savor the flavors of every delicious dish. Take any and every opportunity to taste and ponder. Wonder. Question. Dive deep. Don't worry if you can't figure yourself out. Forgive everyone else for not getting it perfect too.

There is no danger of running out of mystery as far as I can tell. It seems to be built into the 'perception of consciousness' equation. I will contemplate this further in the future.

A word here about honesty, trust, and truth. This idea of mysteriousness and the desire for the unknown needs to match up just so with another phrase that I think most 'good mothers', and probably a good number of other people, end up saying: *"Honesty is the best policy."*
I know, I know.

Gabrielle Angel Dee Lilly

There is some healthy tension between mystery and honesty. Between saying too much and saying too little. Balance is crucial as we move through the mystery.

The truth always catches up. Withholding the whole truth from anyone is really holding back their evolution, at least potentially. That is essentially slowing the evolution of everything. That's fine too. The choice is up to you.

When we lie or withhold the truth, that is different from genuine participation in the mystery. That is manipulation. It is trying to control someone else's ability to process the truth for themselves. It smacks of mistrust and creates anxiety. It grows from fear and insecurity left unchecked. The intuitive, higher-self wobbles around lies. Love fades. Joy dims. Weakness and wobble become the new norm. Societies seem to live in this state much of the time.

Best to try to always be moving towards the ideal of truth. It does sometimes sting, but it might also just surprise you. Deceit is painful, and not delightfully surprising to anyone. I vote 'no' on dishonesty and deceit, for the record. Pretty much across the board, through the gamete, and up and down the entire spectrum, I think honesty is always the best policy.

To the beat now.

Do your best to be honest, even if you are afraid it will hurt. Sometimes it will hurt. You never can tell. That is part of the mystery.

Even when it goes as bad as the worst you can imagine, and everything gets wrecked. Even if people cry, nations crumble and die. Still, even then, the pain and hollowness of living a lie, living a life of mistrust and misalignment with your own word, is much worse than any pain that telling the truth is likely to cause. That is my strong opinion, and many a wise philosopher and mother has agreed with me, throughout history.

"One is never afraid of the unknown; one is afraid of the known coming to an end."
~Jiddu Krishnamurti

Gabrielle Angel Dee Lilly

"Beneath the Looking Glass"
~Angel Lilly, January 2019

truth eight

"Growth hurts."

Sometimes. It's not so much painful really, as it is uncomfortable. Unfamiliar. Scary sometimes. When we grow, we have to let go of our old sense of self and expand into the unknown.

Depending on what time scale lens you look through, and when you look, the growth, the unfolding, the bloom, is often beautiful to us. It can be delightfully surprising, colorful, dynamic. It can also be chaotic. Full of tension. It can seem very disorganized from the outside, or from the inside. It all depends on your perspective.

Growing is, more often than not, more about discomfort and disruption, than comfort and success. The mountain top is awesome. The degree. The financial goals. The dream trip with the dreamy family. All awesome, and worthy of your focus to achieve. The growth though, that good stuff, the real heart of the matter, that is in the climb, in the daily grind, in the classes, the work, and the planning. It helps to keep this in mind when the discomfort seems overwhelming.

Be sure to keep a toolbox full of smiles and laughter and lightness in and around you all along the way. Enjoy the grind of it, as much as you can.

When you feel uncomfortable, it could mean you are growing.

There are different types of comfort, and different types of discomfort. You have to learn to recognize between the discomfort of the unfamiliar, the discomfort of learning new skills, and the discomfort of going against what you think is really right, getting misaligned. That later part is the part to avoid as much as you can. That first part; move towards more of that.

Follow your heart. Well, once you learn to recognize where, or more accurately, how it is leading you to go. You can feel it, with practice. Sometimes it's quiet though. It's calm, steady, and confident.

Imagine the swimmer who learns to hold her breath underwater for 2 minutes, or the race car driver who loves the feeling of her body just barely holding itself together as she speeds around a corner at some insane velocity, or the poet who becomes a professional speaker at corporate events even though she trained to be a lawyer, or you, becoming whatever you want to be.

Imagine the discomfort a snake or dragon or hermit crab must feel before it finally scratches off its old skin to reveal a fresher, larger, more mature version of itself. Similar to that, you must get comfortable with some types of discomfort, and learn to minimize others. If you want to live fully alive. That's my opinion.

Don't get cooked. Stay warm. Keep Cool. Grow.

Forgiveness is the key to dissolving the pain of growing. The ego does not know the difference between transformation and annihilation. So when our identities, our old stories are threatened, we often fight back as if we are fighting for our lives. This often leads to lashing out, hurting the ones we love, including ourselves.

Forgiveness is not for the forgiven, unless you are forgiving yourself. Forgiveness releases the harbor-er from the hurts of resentments, the weight of shame, and the disempowerment of blame.

I continue to practice and learn the art and science of letting go at just the right time. When to hold on and when to let go is an individual thing. There really isn't a right or wrong to it, thought there does seem to be things perfectly timed. We often try to speed up the growth of things with fertilizers or stimulants or other methods of manipulating the circumstances and environments we are in. In my experience, any gain you may get in one area is usually offset by some limiting factor or bottleneck somewhere else. Everything unfolds in its own time.

In my childhood there were many litters of puppies and kittens. If you have ever been around a newborn litter, you know their eyes remain closed tight for days or weeks after they are born. I was often impatient as a child, and several times I pried open the eyelids of puppies and kittens a few days before they were probably ready. I don't know what effect that had, except to remind me now that it does no good to rush things. Puppies will see when they are ready. Even if they do see the light a few days sooner, so what? I imagine people are the same way. It probably does no good to pry their eyelids open before their time. People can only see when they are ready.

*"Change your thoughts
and you change your world."*
~Norman Vincent Peale

"If you desire ease, forsake learning."
~Nagarjuna

=

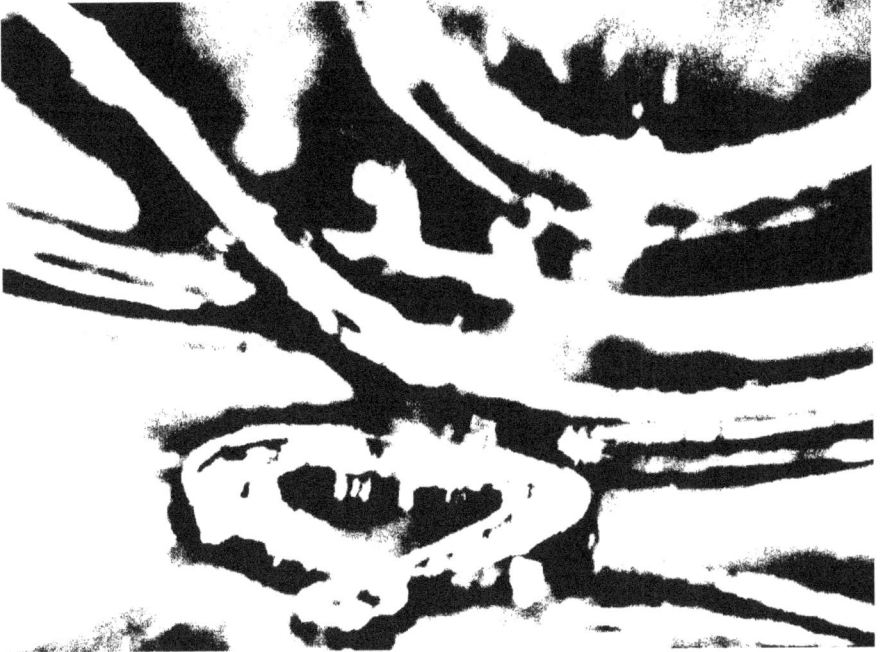

"Swimming Heart"
~Angel Lilly

Gabrielle Angel Dee Lilly

"Time discovers truth."
~Seneca

number nine

"You are making it harder than it has to be."

Yeah, okay. Sometimes we like it hard. Lots of reasons we might. A few things are better hard. Ahem.

Mostly, we seem to think things are better if we have to struggle to get them. We love the underdog, so we sometimes think 'tying one arm behind our backs' will make our victory all the sweeter.

Also, we fear success. More than failure, in my experience, since failure leaves us free to do nothing much, other than join the herds, add our complaints to the complaining buckets. Same nothing we've always done. Eat our slop and die slowly in well-deserved discontent.

We get crabby and drag each other down, like crabs are known to do when they are trapped in a pot together.

We hold each other down, and we get in our own way. We hobble ourselves. Or, my very least favorite, we play the *'look what you made me do'* game, and find someone else to blame for our struggles, our discomfort, our stagnation, our ruminations. Our banging our heads against walls.

Gabrielle Angel Dee Lilly

"Look what you made me do. I've ruined my life and it's all your fault. I broke my hand on the wall because you made me so angry. I wasted my youth supporting you. You bring out the worst in me. You made a liar out of me. You made a fool of me. You made me smaller than I could have been."

We spent lifetimes making up excuses and lame stories about why we never bought the ticket or took the ride. *(That's a Hunter Thompson reference...is that a bad example?) It is what it is...Am I overthinking this?*

Don't overthink it.

> *Let go of the past and drive forward.*

Blaming and shaming ourselves and others doesn't do anyone any good. We make up excuses and endless stories about why we can't or didn't or shouldn't, instead of trying the new thing and finding out if we want to continue or turn around.

Often when we do take the ride, we side on the wrong side of ourselves. We bash against the edges, swim against the flow. We kick and scream and resist. We hold on to old notions and obsolete boundaries, shouting out old shit stories so loudly we can't hear the drum, the hum, the heartbeat of the real dance. The new hotness.

Your true beat. Your dancing feet, they know just how to step, just when to turn, how to carry you home, to the ocean, wherever you desire to roam. Some of this living alive stuff is quite challenging all on its own. Not much need to make any of it any harder.

> *Everyway is the right way when you are dancing.*

The good part of this is, you can find great clues about where you are getting in your own way by looking for patterns. Patterns in your life are there because you are repeating things, or they are part of natural cycles. In any case, it's a good idea to look at them once you notice them.

How are they playing out in your experiences? Are they still serving you like they used to? What are you getting from them? Can you get that in a better, healthier, or more direct way? Is the story you are telling yourself really true? Does it sound good to you? What are you willing to change? What feels right? What is trying is to emerge? Why?

Examine any pattern you recognize and decide if you want to keep carrying it with you, or if you would travel more quickly, joyfully, or easily, by letting it go. And if so, just let go. Put it down. Unpack it if you want to, though you probably don't need to. In any case, then leave it. Don't pick it back up again. That is the other silly thing we do.

The weight of old stories and patterns can become enough to drown an entire country, maybe even a whole world, if carried on long enough past their 'useful before' or, 'up until' date. Make a regular habit of releasing whatever is weighing you down. Like washing your feet and your ass, getting rid of crusty old beliefs and outdated ideals and ideas regularly is important for a healthy, happy life. Especially if you want to keep that fresh feeling.

Some patterns and habits serve us well, and we would do well to focus on building on those for improvements in all areas. Cultivate and develop and build upon what works. Leave the rest behind like it was yesterday.

Gabrielle Angel Dee Lilly

"The difficulty with this conversation is that it's very different from most of the ones I've had of late. Which, as I explained, have mostly been with trees."
~Douglas Adams

"Behind the Grind"
~Angel Lilly, January 2019

Gabrielle Angel Dee Lilly

the tenth truth

"Playfulness Trumps Cowbell"

Ready? Set? Play!!!

Christopher Walkin and Will Ferrell made the iconic phrase "More cowbell!" a garage band staple. I submit that playfulness is really what makes even cowbell work, when we look behind the curtain. In every aspect of life, it is a safe bet that you can benefit by adding more playfulness.

Of course, playfulness has a few tricks up its own sleeves, so to speak, so, I am not so naive as to suggest that if you add more playfulness to every aspect of your life, that it will always be clearly the very best decision, and bring you all the best outcomes, from every possible perspective. Too many factors in this equation for me to be remotely sure that's true. Plus, I probably don't even know you.

Naaa-a-ay. I am proposing that more playfulness is a missing ingredient in many corners and back alleys of life, and also, that it is the type of element which, once added and incorporated, is usually enhanced by adding even more enthusiastic emphAsis on it.

Subtleties disregarded for the moment, at the very least, YOU will have more fun if you do it right. Most likely others will enjoy it too. I'd bet on it. Overall, I vote for more play in all things, every day. I dare you to.

I am aware it could, much like a cowbell, end up being used with the intention of overplaying or disrupting, and in that case, well, that borders on maliciousness, doesn't it? Which, I suppose I should distinguish, is not the kind of playfulness I am referring to. You know what the fuck I mean. Jeez.

Feeling down? Play! Feeling bored? Play! Tired of work? Make it a game! Tired of church? Have a play! Uninspired? Out of shape? Get outside and play! Cat got your tongue? Don't worry, just play! Got a date? Angry at your mate? Play! Play! Play! Why not make life more fun for everyone?

This may be my life's purpose. Adding more play. You will find lessons easier to learn, relationships more pleasant, business more refreshing, and every other aspect of your life better, if you add more playfulness to it.

About a year ago, I read a book called "Your One Word", by Evan Carmichael (2016), and did the exercise in the book to find my "one word". That is supposed to be the one word that sums up everything you do. The word behind the curtain. Similar to Simon Sinek's "Big Why" (2016), it is meant to help focus all aspects of life.

Gabrielle Angel Dee Lilly

At first, I settled on "Voice", "Heart", "Love", and "Spark" as my one word-s. I went through many more after that. Apparently, I am wordy. I ended up making a board with hundreds of my favorite words on it. Lately I have been liking "rawlicious" and "playful", though "curious", "adventure", "celebration" and "relax" are all forefront too. I guess the point is just that I enjoyed the process—or that I am still enjoying the process, and I am not dead yet. In fact, I think I am not even mostly dead, most of the time.

Do you have one word that is at the heart or core or foundation of everything you do? Do you want to?

If you had to choose one word to represent everything you do, what would that word be?

"Things derive their being and nature by mutual dependence and are nothing in themselves."
~Nagarjuna

"One Voice"
~Angel Lilly, January 2019

truth eleven

"We Are Social Animals"

For better and for worse, we are wired to respond to each other, resonate with each other, harmonize with each other, and design lives with regards to one another. Our first experiences of 'self' are through our own reflection in the faces and responses of others. Those of us who choose to live 'on the fringes' of societies mainstream do so at the expense of the peace of mind that comes from sleeping at the center of the pack.

We are also individuals, so we can choose to do that. I find it stimulating and interesting, that we are so wired to pursue our individualism, our uniqueness, and also so neurologically wired to care about our roles in society. We may not want to care about what other people think of us, but what we think other people think has a profound effect on us.

Your purpose is not be loving and kind. Your purpose it to be love and kindness. You are life, discovering itself through its own consciousness. You get to be an individual, and part of a collective. Groups.

Have you have ever watched a swarm of honey bees or a murmuration of starlings, or a school of stingrays shoaling in sync? Have you ever fallen into synchronicity with your fellow humans while playing music or snowboarding or dancing or making love? If you have, then you know something of the wordless, 'no-mind:one-mind' connection which some animals share when they are moving together, especially in-close or fast. We stop being individuals who think for ourselves and we act as part of a larger whole. It is not wholly conscious.

There is a growing body of evidence to support the idea that having a healthy social life is vital to your health in all other areas. Rather than resisting this, becoming a hermit, and making yourself another hard to love, or a hard to get along with person because you got hurt, why not embrace this aspect of your nature? Try it. You might like it. It can be fun!

Find ways to enjoy being social. Connect with the people you want to spend more time with. Cultivate healthy relationships. Do things around other humans, even if you don't have personal relationships with them. Ride the bus. Go play outside with other people. Join a band or a dance class or a sports team. Build or join peer groups around some of your interests. Participate in group activities sometimes. Walk sometimes out on the street where other people walk. It's good for you.

Gabrielle Angel Dee Lilly

There is something about seeing our own reflections in each other that can give us perspective on our own lives that seems impossible to get otherwise. We just can't see ourselves through our own eyes like we can through the eyes of another. To be seen by another is one of our most fundamental needs. To spark a smile in another with our own smile is one of our greatest delights.

We need each other on lots of levels. As infants, middle aged folks, and as aging seniors, each stage of life offers us opportunity to give an receive love in different contexts. We get to try out different sides of all sorts of relationships. Do your best to give generously and receive graciously. What more can we hope for from each other?

"At the end of the day, humans are social animals and we are at our best when we get to do things with others who appreciate and enjoy what we enjoy. It's what keeps us human."
~Simon Sinek

truth twelve

"Extraordinary results correlate with extraordinary actions."

This is one where many of us get it flipped around. We confuse extraordinary with extra-hard or extra-unlikely. If you examine the lives of people you admire, you are likely to see examples of their own, unique, extraordinary actions, which they often took against improbable odds, to reach extraordinary results. Usually the reality of their actions was lots of smaller, seemingly ordinary actions. It's the order, the timing, the repetition, and the juxtaposition which pushes some things into the realms of extraordinary.

Pay attention to the subtle, yet crucial differences. It is not the ends, it is the means. Your uniqueness. The thing that is you, and only you. That is extraordinary. Put THAT into action, however it feels right by you, and you will achieve the extraordinary. Improbability is a bonus in many cases. If you haven't read the Hitchhikers Guide to the Galaxy, well, hopefully there is still time.

Many people I admire and consider successful humans, for example, Gary Vaynerchuck, Tom Bilyeu, Richard Branson, Seth Godin, Oprah, Gabrielle Reese, Marie Forleo; they all put in extraordinary efforts, and got extraordinary results. They did not follow the regular path. They made their own way.

There is something simultaneously extraordinary, incredible, almost unfathomable, and also, something so natural, so unsurprising, so in-line with their unique natures. They are fully and unapologetically themselves. That is what gives a person potential greatness, in my opinion, their regular, everyday, inescapable uniqueness. Find that and you will be on your own, uniquely extraordinary path.

Most of us won't be extraordinary at most things. Some of us won't find anything we want to do the extra work for. Maybe at one thing. Certainly not at everything. I mean, then that would be ordinary. You see the dilemma. It takes extra effort, extra work, extra time, extra ingenuity, extra luck, to reach extraordinary. We wouldn't want it any other way.

This book is a great example of this. I have said "no" to many holiday plans and outings this season, and over the last several years, in order to get this done. Every time I chose to focus my energy on this, instead of something else, even though it was not yet a well-formed idea, it became a little more concrete.

Right now, I can feel all my efforts and time coming together in fantastic ways. Loops closing all around me, quickly. Teasing me with its own great potential to be extraordinary. There are many factors in the extraordinary equation though, when it comes to history and the masses. I am excited to see what this will be. It is impossible to know exactly what things will become in the context of history. We can only be what is extraordinary to ourselves, ultimately. Leave the rest to rest.

Like the sun organizing itself in our solar system, even though it is such a massive, complex, ball of amazeballs and awesomesauce, I mean, fission...is that right? To me, just another self-organizing system, just a different level of super organism, electromagnetically connected to all of everything. Just like you and me. I wonder if it ever does fall in love.

"I don't have to chase extraordinary moments to find happiness - it's right in front of me if I'm paying attention and practicing gratitude."
~Brene' Brown (2016)

Gabrielle Angel Dee Lilly

"Spanish Broom Blooms"
~Angel Lilly, December 2018

*"A truth that's told with bad intent beats all the lies
you can invent."*
~William Blake

"Man is least himself when he talks in his own person. Give him a mask, and he will tell you the truth."
~Oscar Wilde

the thirteenth truth

"Love should be blind. And yet it sees."

In the movie Frida, when Frida asks her father "What is the secret to a happy marriage, Pappa?" he answers: "A short memory." and then in the follow-up question, "Why did you marry mother, Pappa?" "I don't remember." This is one of my favorite dialogues about love, or at least, marriage. Which I suppose brings me to the real point.

Love.

Love is a kind of Universal language, I think. The word only points at things, and it points at a lot. Love is one of the very biggest words there is. Even bigger than "fuck", by a long shot. Love sees everything. Sharply, out in the distance. In close. It smells the truth. And it overlooks anything that does not please. It is important to turn our eyes soft when we think about love. When we say love. I aim to use my vision softly when I look through the filter of love.

Softly now. Not harshly.

Gabrielle Angel Dee Lilly

I know very well how harsh that vivid vision can get. I practiced looking for cold hard facts a large part of my life. And I found plenty. Facts are not always helpful in every part of a good story.

Love is a delicate, fragile, and resilient thing. You can't kill it, but you can easily chase it away. Left alone, it can fade. Love seems to me, a great, and very large part of The Great Mystery, as it should be, and as I believe we should hope it will forever be.

"Parts of Me"
Angel Lilly, 2019

Gabrielle Angel Dee Lilly

Some say love you are what you love. Some say you are
what loves you. What does love mean to you today?

"By Love I See"
~Angel Lilly, 2019

truth fourteen

"Sia writes a pop song in 45 minutes."

Timing matters.

This is dragon energy to me. I'm curious, what do you think of 'dragon energy'? Time and space are bendable in the midst of true greatness. When you get really good, you can flex it. The 'regular rules' do not apply.

This one just got tossed into the pile a few weeks or maybe even just a few minutes ago, and I don't know if it is actually true, though it articulates something I have grappled with my entire life. I did see Sia in an interview where she was sharing her creative process and she said it takes her and her piano player about 45 minutes to write a hit pop song.

The point is, there does not seem to be a direct input-output correlation between effort and quality. No direct, definitive correlation between time-spent and success-of-outcome. At least, not when it comes to pop songs.

Gabrielle Angel Dee Lilly

Not for a lot of other things either. Oh sure, there is some vague correlation between time spent and mastery. Ten thousand hours and all that. Many people spend entire lifetimes never writing any hit pop songs, for example, and some are not even trying. Some do try though. Some try for a long while, and most never really succeed, by their own standards, or by society's standards.

Some of my best; or at least, most catchy, accessible, universally-liked; more likable songs, are those written in one night. Pulled out of the night sky or the ether. Pushed by the moon, or sometimes the afternoon, or even some bright morning sunrise. Caught by the tail or the top of the head. Sometimes lightly, playfully, naturally. Sometimes stubborn, heavy, almost with dread.

I think most creators know that creation comes to and through us, not from us. It is not of us solely, though it is of our soul. Whatever that means. Current science calls it 'flow'. I am not sure what the kids, or the nuns, are calling it these days.

That's the kind of 'waxing poetic' that can just pour out of a person when they get into the flow and let go. Fingers fly. My mind hums in perfect time. Tapping out words and melodies and tricks of phrase. Tapping out meanings and connections and universal truths. Dripping like honey into cups of tea from spoons all over rooms... Nope. Not quite like that.

The other thing. You know what I mean. Yes. That.

The best things don't take the longest. The worst things aren't always the quickest. Correlations between True Creative Genius and time and effort are all topsy-turvy. My guess is that true creative genius; or the muse, or the dragon; resides in another dimension. One where time and space, as we are crudely aware of them, do not apply, at least not by the same rules. Maybe they stay where my dragons lay …Sleeping...Dreaming...Stirring...

Laughing and tumbling with the muse.

"I love the idea of how fast can we make the song, but I don't think that I'm necessarily, like, a super-talented songwriter. I think I'm just really productive. One out of 10 songs is a hit."
~Sia

Gabrielle Angel Dee Lilly

"Petunia Perfection"
~Angel Lilly, December 2018

truth fifteen

"It's Alright to Be Wrong"

Leave some room for uncertainty.

"You don't know, do ya?" Robert Baca (RIP)

That's a good thing. Because being wrong feels exactly like being sure you are right. The most common times that people turn out to be embarrassingly wrong, is just about the time they are totally sure they are totally right. Certain they know the whole answer.

Maybe you don't want to know? Be careful what questions you ask, for questions can be the most powerful transformers. Like magic carpets, questions can sweep you off your feet, change your whole perspective in a minute, and drop you from high places.

Ouch.

Yes, sometimes questions, or rather, the answers to questions, can be painful. Perhaps it is better not to know? I always like to find out. In the long run, I prefer the whole truth.

Questioning your certainties is an important part of a life well-examined, though I question whether or not it is an important part to leave out of a life well-enjoyed.

Overthinking and rumination are the cause of most human suffering, after all. Did I mention that earlier in the all-made-up part? I meant to.

Overthinking is not what I am encouraging you to do. When you catch yourself ruminating, or overthinking, I encourage you instead to knock it off. Stop that. Move along.

Leaving room for questions. Entertain the possibility that you might not have all the facts, you might not be completely or even partially right, you could always have it partially, or even completely wrong. This frees you up to believe whatever you like, since you can, at the same time, not claim it as your certain, capital "T" Truth. After all, certainty is certain death of the exploration of an idea.

There are delicious tastes you have not experienced. There are thoughts which are so brilliant you have not yet developed the words to think. The ocean is still deep.

*"Be not ashamed of mistakes
and thus make them crimes."*
~Confucius

Gabrielle Angel Dee Lilly

"What you don't know is…"
~Angel Lilly, January 2019

truth sixteen

"There is only one story."

The details change. The numbers are arbitrary. And they matter too. Every little detail adds up to the beautiful end. Every speck of spice plays a role in the final flavor. Every note adds to the song. It is all just a fantastic dance in the end. A contest of tensions. A juxtapositioning. The quickening. Only not in that "there can be only one", Highlander kind of way. More in the "we are all one" kind of way.

The story is all simply (are you ready? Too soon? You can skip ahead if you don't want me to spoil the ending already) The Great Unfolding. The mysterious and yet predictably unique, bloom. The slow and sudden dying. The in-between and the all things. The nothing next to nothing next to something.

The words, the names, the details change endlessly. There is no end to it, 'Cotton'. That's a Dodgeball reference.

Gabrielle Angel Dee Lilly

The names, the details, the characters, the directors, the settings; all that stuff changes. The unfolding. The bloom and the decay. That just happens. Naturally.

It's fucking nature, man.

Life, living alive. Call it whatever you want, *"just don't call me late for dinner"*, as my mom used to say. Or was that my grandma? This is one of those beautiful parts for me, where the story is revealing itself through itself. Ben fucking Stiller. Hahahaha. Yeah. It took me a bit to put together who Tom Bilyeu reminds me of. I am sure he has heard it before, and not sure the comparison would bring him any joy. Maybe it would though. You just never know.

THAT, is to 'fUNny', like Matt Damon is to 'potato'. You don't have to get it. We all have our own McDonalds. We all have our own Mat Damon. We all have our own potato. Those are just things that stand in for other things. Ideas and feelings that need opposing words pointed at them to hint at their true meaning. Ideas that are bigger than the words we point at them. Sometimes because we are lazy. Sometimes just overwhelmed. Sometimes trapped. Hurt. Just having fun.

This part should probably be about archetypes. You can play different characters. "Fuck, fight, or hold the light." My late friend Leif used to say. Sometimes mentally I add, freeze, flee, fumble and--did I just add fart? That is silly. I must be some kind of silly fool. Seriously though, even those are all made up. We just keep making things up. It's kinda' what we do. It's all the same story though. If you listen carefully.

Tension, and relax.

It. Not it.

Lost. Found.

You get to make up your own versions. Color it in however you like.

A good friend of mine recently told me he taught his daughter that "life is a shit sandwich. You have to eat a lot of shit before you get any bread, so you best take big bites."

Since I am an incorrigible smartass, I had to point out that there are a lot of things you cannot control in life, but what you put in your sandwich is not one of them. Eating shit sandwiches is just silly. Make your sandwiches however you like them, and then savor the flavor of every single mouthful.

"No, what he didn't like about heroes was that they were usually suicidally gloomy when sober and homicidally insane when drunk."
~Terry Pratchett, The Color of Magic

Gabrielle Angel Dee Lilly

"StarFlowers; Blue and White"
~Angel Lilly, January 2019

truth seventeen

"Sweetness is in the little things."

How you do one thing is how you do everything.

Those little things you do, your small actions, add up to entire days; which add up to your entire lifetime. Pay attention to those small details, make them sweet, or salty, however you like. The rest will follow.

It's easy for someone like me, with a big vision for peaceful global domination, to get overwhelmed by the big picture, miss the trees through the trees. Both are important. Forests and trees.

Let me just pause for a second here and mention, I really love trees. Really, really. I could do a lot more little things to make that love a sweeter demonstration. Okay. Un-pause.

It's important to pause and look your lover in the eyes sometimes. Pause and smile. Pause and take a deep, deep breathe. Let it go.

Gabrielle Angel Dee Lilly

Drop your shoulders. Let go of yesterday. Get jiggy with the present. The more we do that, the more sweet becomes the entire pie.

It might not seem like the sweetness, however. Regular maintenance, upkeep, new paint, clean desks, washed dishes, made beds, fresh sheets, quick smiles, little touches, those are the sweet threads a delicious life is woven of. Knitten into? Kittens? Wait.

I don't know how to knit and I am not sure how to spell crochet. I do know how to crochet though. Last time I checked. These days, any of us can learn anything, anyhow. The point of all of that is to enjoy whatever is at hand. Learn to enjoy the process. Have fun. Play!

It feels good to fix things. It feels good to create. It feels good to figure things out. It feels good to peel off the old skin and begin again. So, here we have it. The little things. So sweet.

Your environment affects your beliefs and your state of mind. Your state of mind impacts your actions, beliefs, outcomes, environment, and circumstances. Clean your fucking room, desk, car, kitchen, windows, girl. Clean up your mind and body, and lifestyle, man.

This might be a good spot to get a hot cup of mate, chai, or peppermint tea. Would you have one for me?
Most people have heard of handwriting analysis. It was popular for a while in the 1970's. The art and science of determining things about your personality and subconscious state by evaluating your handwriting. Fewer people have heard of graphotherapy, which is the practice of making deliberate changes in a person's handwriting in order to affect changes in their personality or mood. Both directions work.

There is so much going on in our own subconscious that we are unaware of and don't understand. Time is not so linear when it comes to archetypes of the mind, beliefs, stories, big shifts, or dragons.

What you see is what you expect; based on what you believe. Tend to the little things that bring you joy, calm, pleasure, bliss. You take care of yours. Let the rest take care of the rest.

"Don't quit. Never give up on trying to build the world you can see, even if others can't see it. Listen to your drum and your drum only. It's the one that makes the sweetest sound."
~Simon Sinek

"The sweetest part of a peach is right next to the rotten part."
~G.A.Lilly

Gabrielle Angel Dee Lilly

"Primrose"
~Angel Lilly, December 2018

truth eighteen

"Decide."

"Decisions are binary. Give it a yes or give it a no." (Gary Vaynerchuck)

Value is not a one factor equation. There are often seemingly endless details to consider when we go to make a decision. Cut the crap though.

You can use your heart-feeling-navigation system to help you decide. It's a yes, or it's a no. Pretend you choose yes if you're not sure. Sleep on it. When you wake up, keep pretending that you chose yes. How do you feel?

Or choose no. I don't care one bit, and probably no one else cares very much either. Just decide. You can always change your mind. 'No"s are just 'Yes"s in disguise anyhow. Like hate is just love, underinformed.

Just choose. You may be wrong, you may be right. Most of the time, there really is no wrong or right. Only what's wrong and right for you, right now. Right now. What is your present truth? That's all you got. All you're gonna' get. That's all there is.

Choose and go with it. Things will get better, or they will get worse, or they won't change much. Either way. You will probably learn something. You will probably solve this problem and find new problems, bigger and better problems maybe. Bigger problems and better bills is really the end goal anyhow, isn't it? Right now. Right here. Wait. Just do your best to drive forward. Let all the rest, take care of all the rest.

Oh! Hey! Speaking of binary, I was watching a YouTube video by Anna Akana today (one of my very favorites, if you are not familiar with her work, check her out). It was about how she 'came out' as bi-sexual to her parents and their reactions via a text message and an engraved plaque. I suddenly realized I have not publicly 'come out' as queer and on the bisexual spectrum myself. Or the Asperger's-autism spectrum either.

Anyhow, at the danger of being pinned down with yet another label, or two, I feel inspired by her to make my own official proclamation. I don't think it is something I personally have any burning need to do, however, I think it is important to open the doors for everyone to define their own sexuality, and be comfortable in whatever of themselves they desire and own.

■■

I consider myself neurologically unique. According to the silly pins and labels being used currently by society, I am queer, and I am bisexual, at least to some degree. I only mention it because I think it might help some others of you feel more free to act accordingly. Just be whoever you want to be. It won't kill you. Hopefully. Is it better to die being true to yourself than live inauthentically? You get to choose.

Do you.

Sexuality is a spectrum, or, like a river to me. It can be somewhat fluid over a person's lifetime; like truth. There are countless ways to do it—go at it—see? That just happens naturally for me. No pun intended. There are countless ways to be. I guess sexuality is a bit like music and love, and butterflies and moths. A bit hard to pin down sometimes. Infinite ways to do the same basic things. Beautiful when alive. Absurd when pinned down inside a cardboard box.

It took me until sometime in my 30's to realize there is definitely something 'queer' about me, by most people's standards. Though certainly deep down I knew it earlier on, and I am sure that it will come as no big surprise to anyone who knows me. It just wasn't something I had a name or label for. "Tomboy" has always been the one thrown at me. Still is, frequently.

Nearly all my sexual relationships are, and have been, and most likely will continue to be with men. I lean strongly on the hetero side of life. "I like Dick", as the 'hetero cis girls' say.
I have kissed a girl though, or two…okay, three. Probably.

That makes me, just me. Freely.

■■■

Gabrielle Angel Dee Lilly

I have been called a shapeshifter. I like that. You can call me queer or bisexual if it does something for you. I currently identify as cis and straight, with a strong leaning towards polyamory.

I am glad changing gender was not an option to consider when I was growing up. Sexuality and gender identity is confusing enough without surgical options, for me. In any case, I am grateful that I am all woman. I am curious about a lot of things, including women and men and my own body. I am also grateful for the ever expanding options we are developing.

So, there you go. That is the first time I have said that like that. Publicly, for the whole world to see. It feels good!

Thanks, Anna! Go team!

(Btw, Anna Akana, I totally feel more interesting now. □)

■■■

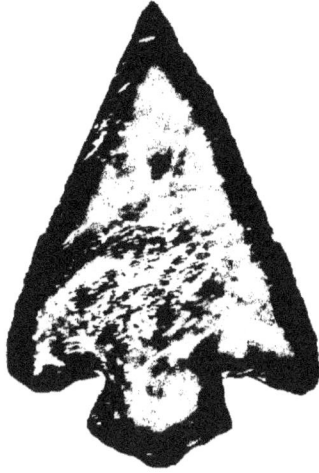

"Time flies like an arrow."

"Fruit flies like a banana."

~Artificial Intelligence/ Oettinger, 1966

Gabrielle Angel Dee Lilly

truth nineteen

"Your dog loves you."

If you have a dog, he or she or it probably does love you.
And a good chance 'your' cat loves you too, if you 'have' a
cat. Everyone else, probably gives less of a fuck about you
or what you do than you would like to think. Maybe you
should give a little less of a fuck too.

Yes, even your dear mom, who probably cares more than most. She just doesn't have time, nor should you hope she does, to make you and what you do her priority anymore. Good chance she thought that was her job for at least a little while when you were younger. Maybe it fucked you both up a lil' bit. No matter though. Just move on.

I hope I didn't fuck up too much, son. If you are reading this, or hearing this. I sure do love you. You gotta' know that. Truly.

Anyhow, even if it feels like no one else cares at all about you, which is hardly ever true, it's still your job to take care of yourself. Love yourself first. Then it will be easier for others to love you.

You are in charge of caring about you, and what you do. No one else is or should be in charge of that. If they are, then I recommend you take a good hard look at that. Unless it's your dog, and then, that seems like a fair exchange. At least, from here.

Really your dog and your cat and your kids probably mostly care about you because you feed them. That's some hardcore medium "T" truth right there. I know it stings a bit. Walk it off if you need to. I'll wait right here.

I am aware this is an area that many of us disagree. I have heard the argument from a good number of people that caring for others is our highest potential, and that knowing someone else cares for you, sometimes more than you care for yourself, can be the thing that saves you. I agree, and respectfully disagree.

Gabrielle Angel Dee Lilly

Good for you if that is true for you. To me, from here, right now, that seems like kind of a cop-out sometimes. Self-sabotage, if you please. The, 'look what you made me do game' cleverly disguised as 'love and commitment'.

Love is unconditional, isn't it?

Partnerships, contracts, ownerships, obligations, relations, those are some of those 'other things' relationships can be. Not love. Love is kind, and relentlessly unforgiving, and calm, and tender, and resilient, and wet-tongued. It's beautiful to me, seeing so many people enjoying successful, healthy, codependent relationships which are mutually beneficial. I really do mean that. Love is messy, any way I look at it.

It's just, not the only way. The codependent way. There is not 'one way' to have a relationship, or one way to love. Every way works, if you come at it aligned with your heart, and put your back into it.

Isn't it amazing that we have so many avocados? If nothing else, that is certainly true.

We are still exploring all the ways we can have relationships. Life love life. No ends are in sight. Only tails wagging. Tales...Anyhow, we should all hope no other brain devotes as much time as each of our individual brains do to figuring themselves out--and the body--mind--toes, nose...all imagined from the dark perspectives of a tiny cavernous wrinkly boney box.

Funny that.

"Outside of a dog, a book is man's best friend.
Inside of a dog it's too dark to read."
~ Groucho Marx

Gabrielle Angel Dee Lilly

"This is Sappy Cat"
~Angel Lilly

truth twenty

"There's not one way."

This is a song I wrote. And a truth I will write about. This might be one of a very few capital "T" Truths to me.

The real Truth here is, "Every Way Works" (Kyle Cease, 2018). Thanks Kyle. This is going to be a T-shirt real soon, I recon'.

Opportunity knocks on both sides of most doors. You can almost always find or make another door. Invent your own way. There are as many paths up the mountain as there are...grains of sand in the ocean? I don't know. I have not done the math on that one.

Gabrielle Angel Dee Lilly

The point is, many choices are just up to you. There isn't one way that is best for everyone. Not one hair style that we all should wear. Thank goodness! Can I get a hello?!? Shout out to Ralph Smiles. We don't all want the same flavor of ice cream every day. Some of us like cookies. Some of us like pie. Some of us enjoy eating the charred flesh of dead baby things sometimes. Some of us like things raw. The point again, is, your way is great. My way is greater. Just kidding. Mostly. Just right now. Just from here. Just to me. Your way is greater for you.

All the ways that work are great. All the ways that don't work are also great, because they help us decide which way the next time. It would be a sad life or no life at all if there was only one right way. I know I said there is really only one truth, and now you see, that truth is infinite. It is the mystery. And it needs diversity. It needs to live, alive. Breathing. On Fire. Not knowing 'the way'. Not having one way. Adapting to every step along the way. Taking in new perspectives. Expanding its own understanding.

We are the way.

There's a story I heard in a video by a builder who inspired me many years ago. Nadar Khalil is his name. I have thought about this story many times over the years. It continues to shift, and I find new meaning in it, which in a way, has become its meaning for me. I think it is also in a book called Sidewalks On The Moon.

The story takes place near a lone tree, beside a well-traveled dirt road. Perhaps the tree is lonely and glad to have the company. I don't know. Maybe it keeps company with the road. Who are we to say?

In any case, in this story, the way I recall it now, there is a professor with no shoes on, standing in the shade of the tree.

A man with a donkey comes by and stops to also enjoy some shade from the tree. The donkey is carrying a sack of grain on one side, and a sack of sand on the other side. The man with the donkey takes off the two sacks to let the donkey enjoy the tree's shade also.

No one mentions how the donkey feels about any of this.

The professor, noticing the sack of sand, asks the man why the donkey is carrying the sand. The man explains it is to balance the weight of the donkey's load, evening out the other side, across from the sack of grain.

The professor is confused and asks the man with the donkey why he does not split the grain into two equal, lesser parts, thus lessening the overall load for the donkey and still keeping the weight evenly balanced and distributed.

The man is confused. He packs up his donkey and continues down the road, muttering to himself silently.

Gabrielle Angel Dee Lilly

The first time I heard this story, I was confused too. This is how I remember it, and it is possible there is some important detail I missed or have forgotten. I may go back and give it another visit one day. Meanwhile, it has served me well as a thing for my brain to crunch on, trying to digest it, take some tasty morsel of a moral out of it.

At first, I thought, it was meant to demonstrate how stubborn people can be. Stuck in our ways. Even when a logical solution or new truth presents itself, and it is clearly easier than the present truth we are living by, we will often choose to disregard the new truth or obvious logic, in favor of our old story. Our identity. The stories we tell ourselves about ourselves are who we are, after all.

Perhaps the professor's lack of shoes was symbolic of his ineptitude. The teacher who I heard this story from was a builder from Iran, or somewhere in the middle east, and so my perception of the story was colored by my filters of whatever that means to me.

Perhaps the donkey needed to stay in good shape so it could carry a heavier load sometimes. Perhaps it was an unruly donkey and the man wanted to punish it or keep it tired. Maybe the man needed the sand.

Perhaps the donkey was really the man's cursed brother or wife and he was carrying out a promise to a mystic or professor or politician or a witch or a warlock to avoid some more terrible fate that might befall them all otherwise. You just don't know, do ya?

Today, I think the man probably had his reasons. Maybe he tried other ways, maybe he didn't. Whatever the case, him and the donkey had a thing. The way he was doing it was working, so fixing it would be foolish. It might not be perfect, but it was functional, and that was all he wanted. He was not looking for a change. He was not looking for progress or improvement. Nothing was causing him enough discontent or discomfort to be worth the effort of doing things differently. He was content to cool off for a few minutes and have his donkey carry twice the weight.

The professor should probably have worn shoes, since the road was presumably hot, them wanting to stand in the shade.

People need to get pretty uncomfortable before they want to change, in my experience.

"It's a damn poor mind that can only think of one way to spell a word."
~Unknown

Gabrielle Angel Dee Lilly

"I'm Just Howlin' For You"
~Angel Lilly, January 2019

Twenty-first century truth

"You can always change your mind."

Begin Again.

This one flows well after the last one, and since my weeks of arrangement have gone right to the wayside today, as soon as I started writing this, what is to be my 'fifth and final first draft' of this book, I will put it right here. Plus, now I can mention the ten or more drafts that came after that. I am currently on 10.6 of the final draft. Make that 11. 12. Hopefully, each iteration is slightly better than the last.

Science is indeed discovering more and more ways we can change. Our brains are more plastic than we, our brains, I mean, than they originally thought. Even our neurology and our microbiomes are turning out to be more malleable than we ever thought. I won't be too surprised when we find out everything kind of is. "We", meaning the published scientific community. The community with immunity to truth. Just kidding. Kidding; not kidding.

Short attention span theater, anyone?

Gabrielle Angel Dee Lilly

Seriously though, you can change your mind, and sometimes you probably should. It is one of the most potentially costly things to do with your energy and time though. A mind, changing itself. I wouldn't do it 'just because' very often. Indecision is the most expensive decision of all though. So, decide. Change your mind later if you feel inclined.

Don't keep holding on to a bad decision just because you spent a lot of time making it.

If you please: Drive forward.

"Embrace the suck."
~Brene' Brown (Dare To Lead, 2018)

"Success is self-defined. You can choose what you think success is, and you can always change your mind."
~Mark Manson (The Subtle Art of Not Giving A Fuck, 2016)

"If you are not embarrassed by the first version you are waiting too long to put it out"
~Reid Hoffman (Blitzscaling, October 9, 2018)

Gabrielle Angel Dee Lilly

"Still Barking at the Moon"
~Angel Lilly

truth twenty-two

"Paralysis is in perfection."

Similar to Medusa, in that it can freeze you, turn you into dull gray stone, hexed, cursed, droned; and different, at least with the snaky hair thing, though that is pretty perfect when I think about it, perfection can paralyze you.

Crumbling analogies aside, it's true that getting caught up in perfection can lead to paralysis, dimming down, dullness, and the like. Over-polishing is a thing. Perfectly polished is nice.

Rawlicious is delicious.

Maybe that's my thing.

Don't wait for conditions to be perfect to make a move. Wait till they are good enough. Move.

Gabrielle Angel Dee Lilly

I had a professor in business school, and who later became my mentor. He was our instructor for the first and the last class in an Organizational Management and Leadership MA program.

On the first day of class he asked us how many of us tried to put in 100% to everything we do. Most of us raised our hands. Some said they put in 110% Then he lectured us on how 80%, or 'good enough' is good enough for most circumstances. You should save your 100% effort for when you absolutely need it. Most of the time, in grad school and in lots of areas of life, 80% is good enough.

That truth breaks down all over the place if you try to apply it to living your best life. Do your best, always. And even when your best is not as good as you wish it was. Do your best anyway. Your best will get better with practice. Sometimes your best will be 80%. Sometimes more. Sometimes less. It's all perfect in its imperfection. It just is what it is. We might as well accept the present and move on. Love it even, if you can.

Hardly anyone makes their greatest masterpiece on the first try. Usually it takes years of practice, and hundreds of failures, and countless 80%'s, and a lot of good timing and grabbing of opportunity--maybe even a little luck--to create anything history will deem as a masterpiece. That does not mean you should not try to achieve mastery status or level. It just means you shouldn't hold your breath.

Take some small actions towards your goals every day. I recommend you start with getting in alignment with your reasons for doing whatever you are doing. Then take action. Play.

Even when you know you are not doing your absolute best, do the best you can from where you are with what you have at the time. Keep practicing and you will get better, or you will quit...or you will die trying. In any case, at least you won't be standing still. Hopefully you won't be complaining.

If you wait for the weather and the boat and every other detail to be perfect, you might never leave the shore. That's a reference to a guy I saw on an interview on Impact Theory with Tom Bilyeu. This guy sailed around the world with his family for two years. It was an epic journey. Lots of his friends made similar plans, yet none of them have started yet. He and his family are already back home, writing books about their experiences and making new plans. Sometimes you just got to leap. Sometimes good enough is good enough. And sailing around the world with your family on a small boat is not for everyone.

"Finished is better than perfect" was my mantra last year. This year I suppose it was just *'do better'*, which worked out okay, I guess. Fantastic, actually. All in all. I did do better, though not more. At least it doesn't seem so, so far. There's still five more days left this year. ...One now. Half of one.

This coming year, 2019, I think I really will finish a lot more, be a lot better, and maybe I won't bother with a--rather, I will choose a perfect-for-now-mantra, ditch it, or transform it if it doesn't work, and move the fuck on. I will.

I have learned that in order to move forward, I must be willing to trudge ahead looking like a fool, falling down, failing, or even, gasp, playing mediocre covers. That's a reference to a garage band I play in, called Kirks Garage Band, or KGB, where we play a lot of mediocre covers.

I did just give my daily Five Finger Mantras a makeover.

Gabrielle Angel Dee Lilly

Want to hear it? 'Like to hear it go':

> *"I trust.*
>
> *I align.*
>
> *I connect.*
>
> *I let go.*
>
> *I play."*

I am positive energy in motion.

I matter.

"Let come what comes, let go what goes.
See what remains."
~Ramana Maharshi

Gabrielle Angel Dee Lilly

"You Are Everything. You Are Enough."
~Angel Lilly

the truth of twenty-three

"Birds in Law "

"Birds of a feather, flock together..." I'm guessing that's because one feather isn't even enough to keep one bird warm, let alone an entire flock. Even if it was a small flock. I will have to look up later, where that saying came from and what it really means. Meanwhile, let's talk about (pause for dramatic effect, dadadaaa) 'the law of attraction'. And also, chaos. Muahahahahaahahaaaaa.
(meniacle laughter for comedic effect)

I imagine some of you feel a little bit closer to me now. And some of you, not so much. This, my pretty pets, is the law of attraction at work. Oh, yeah, and also, chaos.

I do think maybe the co-creators f-ed up a little on this one. Naming it, that is. That's just my slight personal bias, which I feel an urge to get out in the open now. The word "law" makes me a bit squeamish. A little queasy. A bit breezy.

It's exactly like pinning butterflies to boards in an attempt to capture their amazing beauty and uniqueness. Making up "laws" to 'institute' the truth. For justice. And something something dark side (Family Guy)—I mean, aiming at Justice. Ain't it a shame? Such a shame, really. A dirty shame.

Ugly face. Deep breath. Let it go. Okay, I am smiling again.

I still get off track and all wobbly when I deal with laws sometimes. I see this is a land of opportunity for me.

Everything I have heard about the law of attraction seems relatively true to me, excepting or course, that little "law" bit. Semantics. When I really listen to it, in the context of whatever conversation it is being discussed in, (other than amidst the criticisms by Joe Rogan and Gary Vee and Tom Bilyeu, which, in perfect, fantastic irony, they dismiss as they demonstrate) it's simple energetics. Vibration. Like tuning my guitar. There is a science and an art to it. The art is more subtle than the science, and maybe more true. Perhaps it is more important too.

How would we know?

Even though I really don't love the word "Law", in all its uptight rigidity, curtness and hypocrisy...*'I love him and he don't love me'*...oh, wait, that IS a love song...isn't it?

The opposite of 'Law', might be 'Love'. Which do you think is more true?

What the 'law of attraction peeps' don't seem to bring up a lot is that chaos factor. Entropy. It seems to be a 'law' of sorts too. Equally.

So, things vibrationally align. They come together. We come together. Strings resonate. Hearts beat. Vibrations escalate. And then, something stirs. Something stretches or slips or bends or swerves, or curves. Just a little more to the left. Moments of uncertainty creep in. There's a Rick and Morty reference in there. The wobble begins.

Sometimes we get everything right back in alignment as soon as we notice it. Sometimes we get into the wobble, and it becomes its own attraction. We spin off in all directions, some of us puking, now and then, and again.

Go around merrily. Remember when?

truth twenty-four

"We can only meet where we both go."

"It takes two to tango", my mom still likes to say. This sounds obvious. Deep on the surface. Superficial in its depths? Whatever that means.

So often though, we blame 'the other' for wherever we end up, vibrationally and physically, which is ultimately the same thing on different scales, different outlets of expression. Never mind all that. The point is, meetings require at least two of us, and we often meet in familiar places, physically and vibrationally, and emotionally. Again, it's all kind of the same thing on a fundamental level.

We like to blame one another for the way our interactions go, especially in situations where the result is trauma or abuse. Please do not misunderstand me here, I am not saying abuse is good, or that victims deserve their trauma, exactly. I am saying, there is a vibrational alignment in every situation, and we have a higher degree of choice than we are often using. We can learn a higher level of control in our own responses, which can and does change outcomes. It's tricky. She's crafty.

Put that Beasty Boys on the soundtrack; come on. Have a piece of toast. Some crackers with cream cheese.

I am aware this is an anger-provoking stance for some, and I appreciate the controversial aspects of this truth. It's true for me. It doesn't have to be true for you right now. There is room here for more than one truth.

As a victim myself for much of my life, I have contemplated this truth a great deal. Like so many beings, I came into my own sense of identity pre-designed with a victim mindset. My mentality was conditioned from the onset to wonder why I was not treated like other girls, why I did not get what other family members got, why my mom and I never seemed to have enough or be enough, and why I did not have a daddy like most girls seemed to.

I was abused in infancy a little; in all the usual, best intended ways. By some standards perhaps I was neglected in childhood some too, though my mom did an excellent job raising me to be a free, creative, independent thinker.
My father refused to put his name on my birth certificate. My mother was disowned by her father for having me and keeping me out of wedlock. She worked hard to support us as a single mom in the 70's. A year or two earlier and our stories might have been much different.

Measured by mainstream standards, I turned out every bit as 'messed up' as my grandfather said I probably would. I had no clue that women were considered weaker or lesser to men in any way by society until I hit puberty. I believed I was free and wild. I acted accordingly. Even then, and still now, I think I get a lot of things twisted up in translation. I just don't see things the same way most people do. I am regularly grateful for that; even though it has had its cost, like everything does.

A deviation or two from the center of most bell curves; I was never really quite 'right' by mainstream standards. I was incarcerated briefly for a few hours, or days, or weeks, at age 13, 14, and again at age 15. The first time was for having consensual sex with a 23 year old man when I was 13. From my adult vantage point, that seems wrong. At the time, it only seemed wrong of me.

Shame about my sexuality and my identity has always been part of my story. Victimhood was woven into the fabric of my being. I was harassed, bullied, raped, beaten-- lots of things --when I was growing up. My teen years were tough. I took nearly all my lessons the long and hard way.

I have had sex for money, sex for favors, sex to get out of bad situations. I've had sex for love. Sex for affection. Sex because I thought it was what 'my man' wanted. Sex just to see what it could be. I am still fascinated by the creative and transformative powers of sexuality.

So, I have been a thief and a liar. I have tried most of the drugs society says I shouldn't have. Many of them many more times than once. I've bought and sold most all the regular things people buy and sell on the streets. I was raised mostly by wolves and outlaws and arroyos and streams. I have pointed guns at people, and people have pointed guns at me.

The point of all of that is, I know what it feels like to be aligned with various states of being. I know real aliveness. I know real suffering. I know on some level, vibrationally, physically, we must be aligned with what we are experiencing, in order to experience it that way.

I'm not saying any of those circumstances can't still happen to me. I will say they would be different to me now from here than they were then. Like everything.

I wanted to be Robin Hood when I was 7 and 8. I stole boxes of candy and gave it away to 'poor candiless children like me' on the street. Robin Hood or Bugs Bunny. Or Tonto. I wasn't totally sure back then exactly who I wanted to be when I grew up. Some sort of villain hero. Vigilante. A rebel with a cause.

When I was 17 a lot of things happened to me. One of those, was that I was sexually assaulted, violently, by two men with a crowbar and a gun, one night in an abandoned yard in Las Vegas. I was hitchhiking to Lake Tahoe with a friend. We set up camp for the night, thinking we were safe, and woke to two psychopathic criminals who tortured us for some time, celebrating their recent release from prison. My friend was knocked unconscious, and I was taunted and mocked and tortured slowly.

Gabrielle Angel Dee Lilly

While I was lying face down on the ground with my pants torn off and my torn and bloody shirt twisted around my face, I had one of those 'life flashing by' experiences. I thought about how my body would be mutilated and hard to recognize, and briefly wondered 'why'. In that moment, I remembered a time as a child, when I sat and tore the wings off of flies as they crawled around in helpless circles on the window panes. Just to see. Not really feeling. Not really aware that I was being cruel. Maybe vaguely aware. Not conscious or contemplating it though, I don't think. Then again, maybe I was. I can't remember what I was thinking.

That is what these men were like. Me, as a curious and somewhat cruel child. Hurt. Numb. Angry and not knowing why. Wanting power over something or someone weaker and smaller than me. I know what that feels like. I have been vibrationally aligned with all of that. In a daze, a haze of rage and not knowing why. Hurting, and wanting to hurt.

And right now, I am not. Because I say so. I decide, and I make it so. I choose to love. I live alive. Unafraid. Unapologetically. I make better choices. I do the work. I heal. I wake up and I do it again. And again. I show up and stay in the room.

This is the part I hope you can understand, if you only understand one part. You get to decide. You get to make you. You get to choose.

Iffin' it is, or iffin' it isn't, all an illusion; it feels good to choose, make your own way. You get to decide how and what and when to play.

So, set your own boundaries and play. Choose. Line up with what you want, with your 'Big Why (Simon Sinek), your "one Word' (Evan Carmichael) or your One True Purpose, whatever that is. Then get ready. Be prepared for entropy, magnetism, coincidence, synchronicity, and all other sorts of wonderful dance steps along the way. Let's play.

"Let's meet when we both will enjoy being."
~G.A.Lilly

Gabrielle Angel Dee Lilly

"If it's never our fault, we can't take responsibility for it. If we can't take responsibility for it, we'll always be its victim."
~Richard Bach

"Some of the flowers that I am…"
~Angel Lilly

truth twenty-five

"Patterns, patterns, patterns..."

Hey Marsha, watch me pull a rabbit out of a hat. Oh! Wise guy eh?

When you see patterns, those are your reflections. *Oh, hey, what's that smell?* That smell? It's probably you. The looks you keep getting? Most likely, something about you. That thing people keep saying to you? Definitely, probably all you too. Is that bread and butter pickles?

"You can tell it is your problem if it bothers you."

We all have baggage we bring forward from our past. Some of it is just nature. Genetics. History. The stories we get passed down to us through memes and genes.

Natural patterns have a more profound effect on us than most of us give credit most of the time. So, first off, do a biology check. Are you getting good sleep? Drinking enough water? Eating good food? Exercising? Breathing deep? Cleansing and letting go routinely? Where's the moon?

Excepting those rare cases of severe traumatic brain injury or ...no, those are the only cases I know of actually, in or out of the womb...most of us are creating and recreating our stories in the form of an identity, and to a large extent, these serve us very well.

I am not in any big hurry for everyone to 'become enlightened' and loosen their grips on their well-patterned identities. At least, not on most days. I recognize this would be a lot to manage and probably quite uncomfortable for just about everyone all the time.

Patterns and habits give us comfort, predictable themes and phrases to hang our hats and hearts on. They serve us well. Many of them anyhow, most of the time.

Now and again though, seemingly inescapably, one will slip by long after its usefulness has worn out. Like outdated wallpaper, it will be well into the next decade before anyone even looks up long enough to remark on how dysfunctional it has become in the room it's in, and it could be another decade or two before you find yourself in a room or out in a field or in the woods of Colorado or somewhere screaming into the darkness.

Gabrielle Angel Dee Lilly

"Why me?!" Why does this keep happening to me? Why doesn't anyone love me? Why does this always happen?"

And right there, rejoice. Let yourself feel a little spark of joy. You might even let a smile slip in or burst into tears of laughter.

Because right there is your sign.

That is why. Your 'little "w"' why. Your big "W" why.

You are beating the drum of an old worn out story.

All you need is some new wall paper or some deep inner transformation. Something to disrupt the old pattern and create a whole new, better you! (Jay Samit, Disrupt you, 2016).

I know it sounds really easy. It can be difficult though. Tricky. Best to consult your friendly neighborhood coyote or kachina or other trickster magic practitioner, if you know one. And if you don't, it might be high time you get out more and meet one. Or become one. We 'can has' both.

"I stand for wildness."
~G.A.Lilly

truth twenty-six & Intermission

We're just about more than half way through this baby now, so take a little intermission if you need one. No, really. I'll wait. (Cue the music, Alex).

What can we do for an intermission? A song? A dance? A meditation? A story? We can let Grandmother spider decide. A story about dragons perhaps?

Here is something I would like to say about dragons. When I went to business school in the year 2000 (!), In my initial plan, I named my single-operator mail-order company, Sleeping Dragons. I got some flak for that. Many of my fellow students and instructors asked me why I would choose a name that is scary to so many people.

"Dragons are misunderstood", I said. I don't mean the scary fairy tale dragons, though there are tastily toasted tidbits of truth in those images too. I mean the limitless, magic, timeless, transformative power than lies just outside this dimension. Scientists are calling it the quantum field lately, I think.

Dragon energy is that potential which is always there. Ready to rise. Ready to burn. Ready to change everything in an instant; though the time-space continuum is completely different in that dimension, so an instant could take a million more years our time, or, it could already be done.

Truth is, I had a vision of sorts, which was the result of a fantastic incident involving a car-jacked truck, some cocaine smugglers from Cuba, and my front fence, which later became a sleeping dragons wall. That's a story for another day. I don't have to make this stuff up. My life is pretty entertaining. It's true.

Anyway, I've kept the name, Sleeping Dragons, for more than 18 years now. The business was relatively successful for about 12 of those years. It aided and embedded me in purchasing my own home. It helped me to get myself through college and my son through elementary, junior high, and high school as a single parent. Yes, I know it's abetting. Now I do, anyhow, because I have google now. Embedding is what I meant, though, so…or was it imbedding? Gah.

I want to add, when I tell anyone "I had a vision", which I do from time to time, I don't mean I am some mystic or shaman or witch, though who knows, maybe I am. I mean, I get pictures in my head. I can see pictures of things, in my imagination.

Gabrielle Angel Dee Lilly

Envisioning, or, vivid visioning, as I like to call it lately, is just imagining a future I want to create. It does seem sometimes to be co-created through me, by something larger perhaps, that is the feeling I get. I have to decide and then work for it though, if I want it. That is what makes it feel 'visionary' instead of just like regular day dreaming. The persistent and increasingly clear imaginations.

I have a grand vision involving unity, community, kissing dragons, and large dragon energy lately. It involves very large sculptural buildings (Megasculptures), unity, and community-building on a global scale, while still connecting locally. More on that coming soon. I am excited to share that with you in the near future.

Thank you, Dragon. Energy. Unknown potential. Mountains. We sometimes sleep and rise in different time scales and from distant spaces.

Back to the truth. We're on truth 26, in case you forgot.

"A Horse, Of Course"
~Angel Lilly

"Shake it up, baby."

Seriously. I can wait. Give it a good shake.

It's important to disrupt those patterns. Even those that serve you. Examine your routines, freshen them up. Move your body. Twist and shout. I'll wait again. You know what two times 26 is, right? 40 twalve. That's right. Onward.

It wouldn't hurt to start picking up some good dance moves along the way. I'm not saying be a total spaz. Not all the time anyway. You can shake it up and still keep it cool, calm and collected.

You can let it all hang out sometimes too. Try out more than a few different styles and techniques. Go with whatever suits you. Let yourself be uncomfortable sometimes and see how that changes you.

This reminds me of a time I rode my snowboard with my bindings in a fully bidirectional position, 15-22 degrees out on both sides, in a weird horse stance, for a few years.

My riding buddy at the time, every now and then, as we progressed, would say, 'hey, you should try setting your bindings more unidirectionally sometime and you know, just see how it feels. Or even just a little less 'switchy'. Like 7 and 17'.

For years I stubbornly refused his suggestion, knowing with all the certainty of a person in error that he had no idea what would feel best for me to ride, and that my first or second guess on where to set my bindings was what I had gotten comfortable with, so clearly, was probably best for me. Sort of like that guy with the donkey, I saw no reason to fix what was not broken.

Eventually though, one day I tried it. Just a little adjustment.

My riding improved three sizes that day. My heart grew too.

Maybe my ego shrunk a little too. Come to think of it, nope. Any ego shrinkage I experienced was solid offset by my improved and increasingly stellar performance on my snowboard that season. Her name is HuckleBerry, by the way.

I have been rocking that same layout now for another couple years. I just realized I have some new binding configurations to try out in my near future.

Rock stars aren't afraid to try new shit. In snowboarding, they say, *"if you ain't fallin', you ain't tryin'"*.

Back to my point. If a pattern is delightful, then smile, and keep it around. If the pattern is making you cry and scream, then rejoice, you have identified an area you can make positive change in your life. Growth is upon you. Imminent. Immanent. Emminemminant. You can face it, embrace it, run away, try to hide from it; try to drown yourself in water or whatever. Good luck.

Gabrielle Angel Dee Lilly

I don't think any of us can escape our own truth. Once you catch a glimpse of the 'man behind the curtain', you can't un-see it. Once you realize 'the man', is really you, it might be shocking at first. You might resist the whole idea. You will probably grow. You will probably find out you already have the heart, the brain, and everything else you need to make whatever journey you choose of it. You won't have everything. You will get to figure some things out, ask for help along the way, learn new skills, try new cuisines.

In any case, try to relax. Whatever you are going through right now, it will get better, or it will get worse. Or it won't change. And you get to make choices, align yourself, and get playful all along the way!

Lucky me, I was thrilled to see a bit more behind the curtain. As disillusioning and disappointing as it may be at times, the truth does seem to set me free! That might be for another chapter though, we will have to wait and see...my outlaw nature story?

47 truths

Gabrielle Angel Dee Lilly

the twenty-seventh truth

"Begin Again"

Timing matters. You can always Begin Again.

It probably isn't too late to start right now. Life is longer and shorter than you think, my friend. Whatever you want to do, do it now. Do it soon. Start today. If you started before and then failed or just got in your way and stopped, start again. Begin again. Try again. Fail again. "Just stay alive, no matter the cost!" That's a Last of the Mohicans movie reference. Remember that one?

Timing does matter. The order of things does make a difference. Relative size and speed is crucial. Juxtaposition too.

Practice. Practice. Practice. You will get better. You won't get it perfect all the time. That is how it is.

You might get it wrong. Just pause. Breathe. And do it again. Feel the rhythm. Get into the beat. Don't worry too much about what you look like. You probably look a bit foolish, just like everyone else. Close your eyes. Breathe.

Just let the music move you.

You might run out of time before you finish. Better that, then to finish without even starting.

Inaction rarely gets anything done.

Of course, there are things to be said about timing, and as always, I would never superimpose my own sense of timing over your own. You know better than anyone, when the right time is.

You know if you need to rest first, or if you can press on till dawn. You know if you can take a couple deep breaths and carry on, or if you need to sit on the side of the road and have a good cry. Break down like an overheated car that's gone too far. Compose love songs... That's a Sower reference. They are hard to find anymore.

Some things go in and out of style. There are waves. Currents. Trends. It helps if you can learn to surf. Ride the trends. Don't swim against the current so much, unless that feels right to you right now. You have to feel that with your own body. It's nature. You are nature. We are all one. You can feel it. You got this.

You might not make it the first time. You might not be heard tonight. Send it anyway. Just send it. Go. Context goes by. We are on a continuum. The truth of today is not certain to be the truth of tomorrow, any more than all the truth of today is the same as all the truths of yesterday. Truths change.

Catch the wave today.

Hop. Skip. Jump. Leap. Relax.

A pause is the easiest way to get back in step.

Cha cha cha.

Gabrielle Angel Dee Lilly

"This is Happy Rock Face"
~Angel Lilly, 2019

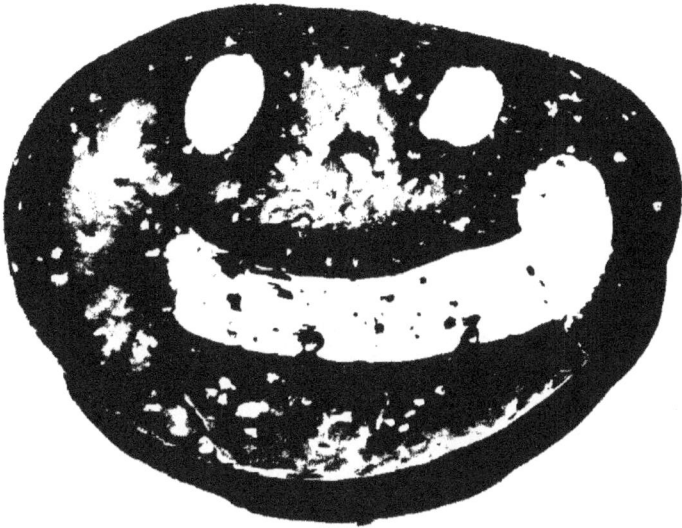

truth twenty-eight

"Happiness is a state of mind."

Is it a warm gun? It's a decision, really. Yes, there is lots of chemistry involved, and all that really comes down to the choices you make too. Deciding to be happy is at least half the key to satisfaction. Is that true? It sounds hopeful anyhow.

I do think happiness is mostly up to us. It is definitely a chemical state, residing mostly in the mind, or at least, originating there it feels like. I am not disregarding the chemistry of hormones, emotional reactions to others, triggers, foods, the list of influences goes on and on and on.

I don't think that most of us have complete control over our mental state or degree of happiness at all times, or even much of the time. I have never met anyone who has, or even claims to have, though a very few do claim to have made great strides towards it. Tony Robins, Joe Dispenza, and Kyle Cease come to mind.

Whatever you believe, it is hard to deny that we can achieve remarkable results when we just decide we are going to. When we refuse to take no for an answer from the universe. Even if you do deny it, what good will that do you?
Here is a poem I like:

"I bargained with Life for a penny,
And Life would pay no more,
However I begged at evening
When I counted my scanty store;

For Life is just an employer,
He gives you what you ask,
But once you have set the wages,
Why, you must bear the task.

I worked for a menial's hire,
Only to learn, dismayed,
That any wage I had asked of Life,
Life would have paid."

— Jessie B. Rittenhouse (1869–1948)
"My Wage," The Door of Dreams, p. 25 (1918).

Dissatisfactions are nearly all illusions. Self-imposed limitations, old stories meant to capture your imagination and manipulate your expectations. Made up conversations.

To realize your dissatisfaction is mostly all in your mind, is to give yourself freedom and power. You can begin to take back a degree of control over your destiny. By controlling your state, you control your point of attraction, which steers you more and more in the directions of following your own path to true happiness.

"The best way to pay for a lovely moment
is to enjoy it."
~Richard Bach

"Sunspots get in my eyes sometimes."
~Angel Lilly, January 2019

47 truths

Gabrielle Angel Dee Lilly

truth twenty-nine

"Nature distracts."

Natural Distractions. "Ooo. Peace of candy" (Simpsons).
People mostly want what they don't have, or what think they
can't have. We want what is rare. We like shiny things. We
don't necessarily like what is best for us. What is your
favorite dessert? I love warm vanilla custard. And peach pie.
Strawberry rhubarb. Chokecherries. Mint.

It's worth spending some time reflecting on the basic (omg)
'laws' of nature. As Robert Greene points out in most, if not
all of his books; there are natural forces, natural inclinations,
behaviors rooted in our nature, which we humans are nearly
all subject to. We are even more enslaved by our own
natural desires when we are unconscious to them, or if we
never acknowledge them at all.

One common trap is to desire things we don't have, especially what others have, for no other reason than we don't have it, or we think it's rare. This is most often triggered by seeing someone else having it. Or thinking of someone else seeing us with it.

Another is wanting things we think others want. It is just part of animal nature to behave this way. To some extent, I think it is good to accept and even embrace it. On the other hand, like anything, better to use it to help develop a life you want and check now and then to see if you are not being a mindless slave to trends of fashion. Unless you are into that sort of thing, and then, by all mean, have at it.

It's good to develop a habit to examine if what we want really serves us in getting closer to our bigger life goals, and our ideal life-well-lived; or if, in fact, as is very often the case, it might just be a distraction, a detour, a detractor, a dissolver of your precious energy. If so, it is probably better left wanted and appreciated for the wanting of it, and not necessarily pursued.

There is a lot to be said for appreciating desire and not needing fulfillment. There is even more to be said about cultivating desire. With our sexual partners, certainly, and with everyday things and all 'betweens'.

When we can learn to really appreciate and cultivate desire for the things we keep in our lives, then, again, we are steps closer to living in that state of bliss, which I will, for now, continue to call the ideal, desired, life-well-lived.

We can have both. Sometimes. If we are willing to do the work. Custard and chokecherry pie? Yup. If that is what you really want. Sometimes it matters not. Or very little. Sometimes, it matters a lot. To you.

Reexamine your big why (Simon Sinek), your main directive, your underlying reasons for doing what you do, every now and again. Make sure you stay on track. The track you set yourself on. Not someone else's or everyone else's. Let them travel on their own tracks. You stay on yours.

Adjust your sails. Get in step. Cha cha cha.

"You know you're driving, right?"
~Snowboarder Scott

the thirtieth truth

"Balance is Boss."

Bawse? King? Queen? Empress? Goddessness? The fool's best tool? Yes, all of that. Balancing opposite forces is a useful tool for less falling down. So is lying on the floor, although that is probably advice for a different book. *"You can't fall off the floor"* is really the punchline of that one. It really hasn't got the stamina for a whole book yet, has it?

Healthy balances are what it is all about; that's what I am saying. Not just because I like yoga. More like, I like yoga because it helps me balance. Anytime I get a sense of balance, I feel like I am doing good. I also like to change it up and find balance in asymmetry. That is a big part of what makes good art to me. Balance without symmetry.

Balance is a good thing. You should want more of it. That is the truth I am presenting to you as my 30th. There is really no reason for it to be the 30th. In fact, now that I bring it up, I am wishing it was number 33 a little bit. That would make some karmic sense and bring a bit more structure and sense of symmetry to this whole affair, wouldn't it? A might bit? Naah. I will leave it be, thirty.

This is the part where I'm gonna talk about creativity and productivity. Not balance. I don't know why I even put that part on this note-card. For now we'll go with it and see where it takes us. Like good creators. Which does iterate and demonstrate my point nicely enough. Productivity and creativity can be on opposite ends of the gettin-it-done spectrum. Ideally, an organization or project or relationship has both. A nice balance of the two, workin' in harmony. See what I did there?

Creativity and productivity are both very valuable parts of the process of making progress the realization of a grand vision. They don't always do best in each other's company, however. I find it is great when I get in flow, and the two halves of my brain work in synchronicity and harmony together, like in writing this book. Sometimes, though, especially on a very large scale or long-time scale project, it is good to give creativity and productivity each their own room, time and space (Shane Snow, Dream Teams).

Sometimes I use the left, more analytical side of my brain more, and other times I am using more of the right side. Ideally, they are working closely together, trusting one another to do the parts each is best at. Really what I am doing is synergy. One dominates, yet, just like in any good relationship, the submissive one is just as important to the outcome, perhaps even more than the dominant one.

Don't look back. You're not going that way.

Gabrielle Angel Dee Lilly

"Everything in moderation, especially moderation."
~G.A.Lilly

"The trick to balance is to not make sacrificing important things become the norm."
~Simon Sinek (2006)

Gabrielle Angel Dee Lilly

"Trinity?"
~Angel Lilly, January 2019

truth thirty-one

"Words are not the things they point to."

I love words. They allow me to write this book. They let us convey ideas and poems and have phonics classes. They are magic. They can change minds and civilizations. Still, like all labels, they fall short of doing everything, all the time. In fact, they are quite silly things which are barely even things really.

Words point to ideas and feelings, places, and faces. They are not the things they point at. We filter out their implied meanings, after they have been carefully or unthoughtful cast out as the pointers we should give our attention to. We follow whatever direction we think or we want from them. All along the way there are distractions, filters, colors, past meanings, attachments, and mis-directions.

The meaning one person derives from the intended meaning of another person's words, is frequently not all that similar. Even when it is very similar, they are still a detached, linear, more left-brain way of thinking. We fill in with images, smells, colors, and feelings. It's the feelings we really remember about where the words are pointing.

Pictures and images also evoke feelings and meanings that are also filtered and subject to the observer. They tend to be less rigid and more open to discussion or expansion of perspective than words sometimes.

When we share our perceptions of a painting, for example, we gain a broader perspective when our descriptions don't exactly match. We try to find words that get closer and closer to our true meaning, and we get closer and close to that meaning in doing so. We share our experience of what it means to us, and explore what it means to others, without so much of a sense of 'right and wrong' meaning which so frequently accompanies the exchange of words.

Let us hope we never fully reach over that horizon, or that when we do, we will see more horizon, looming in the far distance, calling us to quest after it, and so life will go on.

Finding the right words is a science and an art, and I admire those who weave them together well. Wordsmiths like I aspire to be. Still, words only point, they are not the things or places or ideas or feelings they point to.

There is such magic in words, even as the mere pointers they are. The have their own mysteriousness. Their own limitless potential which only becomes finite when we put them down in writing, alongside definitions, under headings, in categories. We fix them in context and then they become particles, instead of waves.

Words call attention to things, people, and ideas; and attention is everything (shout out to Gary Vee). Now that I have pinned these words down in this book, put them in writing, they have already begun to change. Already you can argue with the semantics of them and stray from the intention. The feeling of them changes and starts to fade. And yet, I don't write or publish them at all, then I miss one more opportunity to contribute to this great mystery in my own unique way. This is the one of the great fantastics. Time is limited. It goes by and doesn't come back. That's the rub. It is delicious.

What does this taste like to you? Sweet? Salty? Sour? Bitter? Acrid? Complex?

"The six most important words: I admit I made a mistake. The five most important words: You did a good job. The four most important words: What is your opinion? The three most important words: If you please. The two most important words: Thank you. The one least important word: I."
- Anonymous

Gabrielle Angel Dee

"I Still Love You"
~Angel Lilly

truth thirty-two

"Silence is Golden"

Gold can be heavy or light. It's a lot about perspective. Again, the word silence is not the silence, and the silence says whatever it says and doesn't say. Silence is one of a handful (or maybe it's a whole book...hmmm) of words with magic woven into them. Not in the individual letters of course, I don't think... I mean, the thing the word points to.

Silence lets us fill in, or sink in, with no filling in. Silence is an invitation and a rejection. It is a space-time in which things get bigger or smaller, better or worse. Like the words Love, Fuck, Cunt, Shut-up, Truth, Trust...Silence usually has a lot of weight already thrown onto it and carried around.

People like to do that with the labels we use most. We keep all the meanings loosely attached. I suppose so we can feel less pinned down; use whatever meanings suit us best on the fly.

This makes me think of butterflies, and the current trend to use the analogy of turning from a caterpillar to a butterfly to help describe the process of becoming more self-aware, which many humans seem to be going through. At least, with the internet, and now being able to see each other more, it brings it more into focus. Perhaps it is increasing, or perhaps we are just perceiving more of it in each other. I suppose that is one way for it to increase, isn't it?

When I look back at recorded human philosophy and historical stories, I see a record of the same internal struggle in every one. Same story, different details.

Anyhow, I think of the butterflies we had in school, that we were assigned to collect, identify, and pin down to a piece of cork or foam or cardboard. Display the dead and decaying corpse of what we found beautiful. I always thought that was a cruel joke, and out of respect for butterflies and humans, I refuse to use that analogy to describe our awakening. I will resist! I don't even like the word awakening either. It's evolution, baby.

Life is for the living. Live it alive.

Learn to use silence as the powerful tool it is. Don't allow it to ruin you. Say things that are relevant when they are due. Address tensions in context. Calmly, with some silence between your words. Weave silence in-between your thoughts, and into your feelings. Most of us have a lot of noise clutter going on and not enough silence. Some of us do not speak, or touch, or love, or sing, or otherwise try to communicate well, because the static of this clutter is so loud.

Meditation is often a simple practice of finding silence, or aiming for it.

In my family, 'the silent treatment' was used as punishment, to express disapproval, to train me to behave differently. Attention was withheld when I did not act or look the way my mom wanted to see me. My father never would look at me at all. I developed a strong craving for attention, to be seen, to be talked to, acknowledged. This has served me well at times and other times been something I've thrown firmly in my own way as a limiting belief.

Silence can be heavy, or it can be light. It is powerful medicine in its own right. I advise you to treat it with respect. Learn to read and write in silence. Speak in the tongue of silence now and then. Visit the spaces between where the words point to and just recharge. Pull from the nothing.

There. Better now?

Everybody lies. Maybe you are super-extra-good and you think you only do it on accident. Good for you. You still lie. Most of us have a long list of areas we lie, either consciously or partially consciously, because we don't want to face the truth, or we believe we know what is best in the way of how much truth the other party can 'handle' or has a right to. Even more often, we are completely unaware of the convoluted traps we set ourselves in.

There is silence in the dancing wind, silence in the greenness of trees, and silence in the coldness of snow. Silence in the words I don't say when I have to go.

Also, it's okay to hide when we need to. If you need to hide, try not to lie. Do what you need to do to keep yourself safe though. Just know if you want to ride the big waves, you will need to face you fears, heal, step out of the safe zone, and take the leap into honest living eventually.

We heal to different rhythms, in different times. We can't pry each other out of our hiding spots of rip off one another's armor and expect to be greeted with honesty, openness, and unconditional love. Probably we will be met with hurt, anger, shame, blame, and ultimately, a quick retreat again. Let's practice being more patient with ourselves and each other. Relationships are not perfect, they require presence, and a willingness to be imperfect (Sherry Turkle, Reclaiming Conversation, 2016).

Let's put our phones down and really be together sometimes, when we are together. Let's enjoy our time alone too. Solitude is also golden, when it is what you choose.

Forgive. Let go. Keep healing and move on.

"It's Okay to Cry"
~Angel Lilly

truth thirty-three

"Laughter really is the best medicine."

Remember when I wanted this chapter to be about balance? 3 3's in a row is one of my favorite things. Talk about balance. Anyhow, since this chapter turned out to be about laughter instead, let's get some somewhat dry facts about laughter out of the way first.

Stress causes disease. Laughter reduces stress.

Are you feeling thirsty yet? Laughter is wet. Why do we use that language to point at it? It's juicy. It's nourishing. It helps us open our minds to possibilities.

Educators would be wise to heed these words and consider adding laughter to every lesson. Entertainers already know this very well. Students with their minds cracked open by laughter are much more susceptible to receiving whatever nonsense a professor wants to throw in there then, while the mind is open.

I notice a trend for comedians to become some sort of...mystical guides maybe? Comedy and raising awareness do go hand in hand, skipping down the beaten path, rolling in the grass off the yellow brick road; laughing and testing boundaries. Societies need some of us to be willing to go 'too far' sometimes. How else will we know, where those boundaries are?

Think about children laughing outside on a spring day. The sunshine smells of warm buttercups and clover and sweet-peas. The grass is luscious and not too freshly cut. Maybe the sky is orange...or, blue. It's probably blue, right? Mine can be orange. They are letting go of the past moment, and playing in the right now. How about you?

I like to play. Did I mention that?

"Laughter connects you with people. It's almost impossible to maintain any kind of distance or any sense of social hierarchy when you're just howling with laughter. Laughter is a force for democracy." — *John Cleese, 2015*

*"Nothing exists except atoms and empty space;
everything else is opinion."
~Democritus (c. 460-370 BCE)*

Gabrielle Angel Dee Lilly

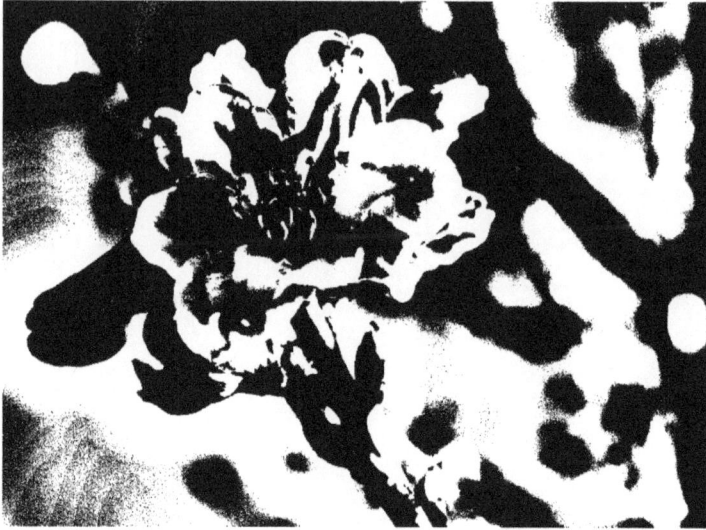

"Joy Blooms"
~Angel Lilly, November 2018

truth thirty-four

"Use what is useful now."

Leave the rest.

It's all well and good to contemplate the grand design or work out the meaning of life and put together a perfect toolbox for every imagined scenario. However, living life fully alive, in the present, sometimes means using a rock for a hammer, a screwdriver for a wood carver, or a matchstick for a toothpick. Those are actually better than 'regular toothpix' on accountta' the charcoal. I'm not 'just sayin' that, it's actually true.

Most of our beliefs run unconsciously in the background, like programs installed long ago. We are unaware of most of the operations going on under the surface which design how we perceive our stories and help us choose which words to use to tell them. It is worth pausing now and again to examine those and make corrections, adjustments in your navigations.

Tighten this sail. Loosen that binding. If what is available to you is not working well, I advise you look at your underlying beliefs and adjust your sails accordingly. Otherwise, and hopefully, most of the time, just stay your course.

There are things you don't understand, and there are things you can't understand. There are things you won't understand. These are different things.

When everything is relatively fine, pick up the right tools for the job at hand, take your best guess at what you will need, trust your ability to make or find new tools along the way, and set sail. Take what you think you are likely to need. Leave the rest behind.

Trust the Universe to meet you when and wherever you are ready.

*"Everyone has a plan
until they get punched in the face."
~Mike Tyson*

Gabrielle Angel Dee Lilly

"Singing Heart"
~Angel Lilly, January 2019

truth thirty-five

"You are stronger than you think."

And more broken.

You can endure a lot more than you think you can. You won't know how much you can accomplish until you push yourself beyond wherever you are sure your limits are.

Human history is full of amazing stories. You can do more than you think, and also, your thoughts are what limit you most of the time.

Feats of strength. Tales of relentless endurance. Outer and inner space. The orchestra. Human history is full of inspiring tales of greatness. Full of nuts and fruit too. It's abundant.

There is an entire Universe conspiring on your behalf. Maybe some of it is unaware that it is on your side. It must be, though—on your side--because you are me and we are everything. I mentioned before that I don't believe in 'god' in a 'conventional' or 'modern' sense. I do believe in a higher sentient order to things. I see evidence of a lot I don't understand.

There are many, many, many things in this life, which are beyond my capacity to understand. I am happy to imagine that there is at least some shared responsibility for creating and running life and Everything, not to mention the potential of the Great Nothing. The point is, not only do you have amazing untapped potential in you; you are also connected to an amazing untapped potential that is this entire Universe. I like to call that Dragon. Mystery. Potential. You. I. All...

Humans, as I mentioned, are these incredible, multi-functional machines made of meat on bone wrapped in skin sacks. We are multi-dimensional. Holographic perhaps. We can learn and do what countless 'man made' machines can do, though no longer everything, for a long while now, with the evolving development of artificial intelligence.

Also, we are wild.

We have incredible endurance. Hunters in the savanna, Frida Kahlo, Bruce Lee, the list literally goes on and on and on. You can put yourself on it if you want to. Nothing about any of those people is more special than you are. Training is a great key for accomplishing what we consider great.

Whether it is writing or running, regular practice, pushing yourself beyond your current comfort zone, is the best way to improve quickly. This means stepping beyond your current limits. Going harder, faster, more than you could before.

Even though our thoughts and beliefs have such a huge influence on our abilities, we can hold space for unknown potential. The mystery. This is where your limitless power lies. This is where I go to find myself when I want to become greater than I was. This is where I would I love to meet you.

"I'm third."
~Jaime Ivey

Gabrielle Angel Dee Lilly

I want to tell you a story here, about a friend of mine; Jaime Ivey. He was my good friend at a time when I didn't have many good friends. He saved my life many years ago, and probably countless other lives as well.

I met Jaime when I was 14 or 15. He had climbed up an electric pole when he was a kid and was electrocuted. His body caught on fire, and a large percentage of his skin was badly burned. He spent two years in and out of a military hospital. There they took the skin from the parts that were not burned and put it on the burned parts. It was a slow, tedious, painful process. I am sure it was terrible most of the time.

As a result of this, he got a substantial settlement from the state of Texas. He had a trust-fund before the age he would have graduated high school. Which he never did.

When I met him, he had his own house in Santa Fe, NM, and a substantial drinking habit to go along with it. I had just run away from home again, to escape another round of incarceration as a juvenile, which, at least back then, was worse than incarceration as an adult. Delinquent juveniles often have fewer rights and are treated with even less respect than criminal adults, in my experience.

Jaime died young, in his late 30's I think. About a decade or so ago. His whole body just gave out. He died from organ failure. His scaring kept his skin from being able to produce sweat, which is critical to help detox the liver and regulate body temperature, among other things. The drinking helped too.

All the years I knew Jaime, even in the last years, when there was more suffering, I never heard him utter an unkind word to anyone. Ever.

When he died, I tried to keep a piece of that part of him in me. I actually accidentally inhaled a significant taste of his ashes at his memorial service, along with most everyone else who was singing that beautiful, windy day.

Last week I asked my good friend Leo, what Jaime's 'catch phrase' used to be. I couldn't remember if he had one. "I'm third." He said. I asked him what it meant. I vaguely remember him saying that a time or two during game nights when we were all around the table playing cards or rolling dice.

It means, "First god, then you, then me."

That sums up Jaime perfectly.

Gabrielle Angel Dee Lilly

"The Road Home"
~Angel Lilly, January 2019

truth thirty-six

"One Breath"

Everything can change in one breath. We recognize a person's or being's first and last breaths as significant. Every breath has the potential to be that significant when we step into the great mystery.

Let go and surrender to the vastness of eternity for a second. Return to the stardust you once were, eons ago, and breathe in the essence of now. Breathe out what was. Breathe in what is and what will become. You decide. You align. You smile. Is that yellow-orange-pink-blue?

Gabrielle Angel Dee Lilly

Real change happens in an instant. Those life changes. Big shifts. Fault lines give way. Fires transform everything back to dust. Mudslides. People and pets unexpectedly die. Waves crash in and wipe everything away. All we can do to prepare is remain calm, strong, and ready to adapt. Ready to leap. And keep breathing.

Breathe in possibility, potential, magic, gold dust, silence, words, feelings, love. Breathe out everything you think you know. Let go. Be. Aubrey Marcus says six breathes can change your state. Whim Hoff uses two minutes, I think. the point is, a lot can change in a breath. Sometimes you have control over it, and sometimes it has control over you. Try to relax.

Breathwork is the simplest, most basic way to return to center. It is right up there, maybe even higher than laughter on the scale of great magic healing medicine. Much like tuning my guitar strings, or practicing the foundations of any instrument, breathing is something we all can improve. Becoming a better breather is the quickest route to becoming a better you. Whatever details you want in your story, I believe this is true.

What will you practice most?

Just breathe. This too shall pass. Change is the only constant. Sometimes it happens fast, in an instant. Sometimes it happens so slow we don't notice it.

"You have a long way to go, so...No. No tired for you." Me

"Ain't nothin' 'round here a nice coat of fire couldn't fix right up." also me

47 truths

Gabrielle Angel Dee Lilly

"Nothing is enough for the man
to whom enough is too little."
~Epicurus (c. 341-270 BCE)

"Apple of my Heart"
~Angel Lilly, January 2019

Gabrielle Angel Dee Lilly

the thirty-seventh truth

"You only owe yourself your self."

Nothing more and nothing less. You are no one else. The best you can hope for is to be the self you want to be. A person who makes you happy. If we all do that, imagine what an amazing Universe we will build.

Whatever anyone else says or does or thinks, you are the one you get to live as, and through. You are the only one you get to be, this entire lifetime. Maybe beyond. The jury is still out on that one. In any case, stay with me for a bit while I unpack this, often controversial truth for you.

Even if you think there is some judgement day, some great creator in the sky, or a tiny tally ticker under your feet, who is adding up all your debts and gifts, summing your generosity and your gluttonies, to come to some conclusion about where you should be filed or marched off to next, which, by the way, seems a very absurd story to me, though no less absurd than most, I suppose, including this one...

Even if you believe that, the complexities of doing your best and trying to be a good person are nearly impossible to sort out with one puny little human brain in a dark boney box. Even if it is all hooked up to the internet and such. A simpler method of being a good person is just to be a good you. Do your best to be a good you.

Be your best version of the unique expression of life that is you. Don't worry that you are not doing it well or you won't be good enough. No one is you, after all, so there is no danger of someone else coming along who is more qualified than you are to do the job of being you.

I feel compelled to reiterate here, that I mean no disrespect to my dear friends, family, and other co-creators yet unmet who hold a belief for or of a god or adhere to religious practices. I see the benefit of this in many lives, and I believe strongly that it is up to each of us to find a story that works for us for now. Religion seems to work for many people, and I love that.

Gabrielle Angel Dee Lilly

I usually can replace the word "God" with "Universe",
"Mystery", "Love" "All" or "Everything" in my mind is we are
having religiously bent conversations, and not get too hung
up on it. I hope you can do the same in the other direction, if
you prefer the more mainstream, or different vocabulary than
the words I am using. These words all point to the same
feeling in the end, don't they?

Vanilla. Chocolate. Sunset. Orange. Deep. Delight. Love.
Magic. Muse. Magnetic. Magnificent. Majestic. Celebration.
Appreciation. Touch. Tree. You. Me.

"The truth is: Belonging starts with self-acceptance. Your level of belonging, in fact, can never be greater than your level of self-acceptance, because believing that you're enough is what gives you the courage to be authentic, vulnerable and imperfect."
~Brene' Brown

Gabrielle Angel Dee Lilly

"You can't escape your nature."
~Angel Lilly, January 2019

truth number thirty-eight

"Music Is Magic"

I don't know how that happens. I nearly neglected to include music in this list. Funny that. Perhaps it is because it is similar to what water is to a fish, what music is to me. Did I mention I play guitar and sing in two bands? That is just one of my favorite things about me. I didn't play or sing for some years in my 20's. I am grateful that I found my way back to it, and very appreciative of the people I get to play music with.

Music has been a magical mystical unifying inspiring moving thread throughout my life. It was my first love. It envelopes everything else I do. Even if it is not musical in the strictest sense, my days are filled with rhythm and rhyme. I notice the repeating patterns, the harmonies, the melodies, the beats. The tricks of phrase.

The meaning of music transcends words.

Gabrielle Angel Dee Lilly

Learning to communicate in the language of music changes a brain, and taps into something primal, something in the subconsciousness. Human understanding of music transcends words, and images, and feelings. It takes us anywhere in space-time, and out of space and time, all at the same time.

I am growing a vivid vision in the works for how to use sound and music to help bring more peaceful communication across cultures and other potential barriers. Music is at the core of nearly everything I do.

Music seems to be the most complex and most basic human language. Closely related to math, the language of music is vibrationally pure. Sound, if you will. Pun intended. Accurate to specific hertz frequencies and patterns; and still fluid, full of infinite potential for exploration, expansion, playfulness and change.

Jazz.

Music might be a capital "T" Truth all on its own. Similar to Love, Music has many, many layers of meaning attached to it. The majority of them are positive.

Music has been my only friend at times in this life. For me personally, it has been a constant guide. A gauge and a modifying filter for the decade to decade, year to year, and minute to minute feelings of my life.

Our history has a soundtrack.

I love the way music and art through history reflects the ages it is created in. I suppose that is how one knows when you are creating something great. When it transcends the artist, and represents the time and space the artist is in. I feel that way about this book. There is something musical, mathematic, lyrical, and beyond me about it.

I can't think of any personal relationships I have or have ever had which I have not viewed through the filter of music somehow. What kind of music a person listens to, or plays, informs us about what kind of person they are. Songwriters tell us even more, I would say, though that is probably because I am a songwriter. We derive a lot from the music we listen to, and how we listen to it.

This is not just a love song, and it is not just a tribute. It's a little of both. Simple math, and complex music.

We can have both.

Gabrielle Angel Dee Lilly

"One good thing about music,
when it hits you, you feel no pain."
~Bob Marley

*"There is geometry in the humming of the strings,
there is music in the spacing of the spheres."*
~Pythagoras (c. 570-495 BCE)

Gabrielle Angel Dee Lilly

"Our hearts are connected."
~Angel Lilly, January 2019

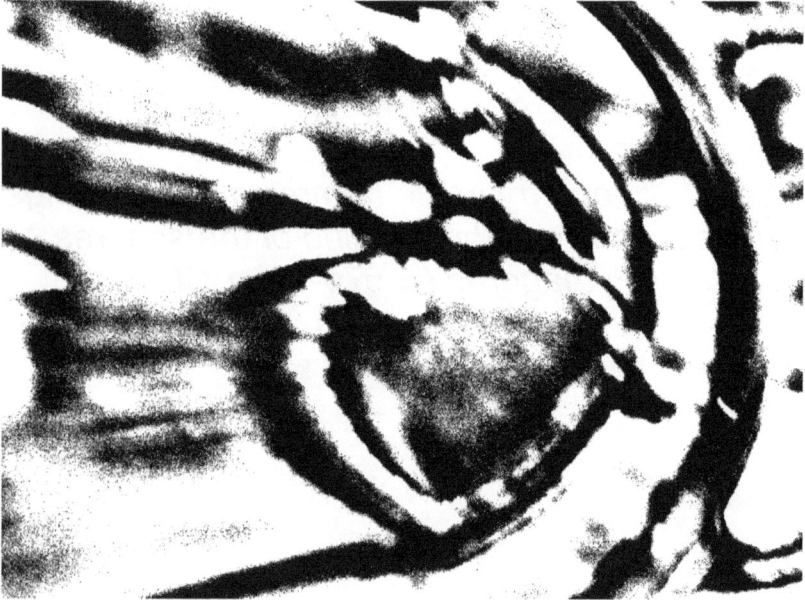

truth number thirty-nine

"The Loop Around"

Yes, it is pretty similar to 'the reach around'. "What comes around, goes around." Just a little different, maybe. It's also similar to the familiar concept of karma. Only, to me, karma is an instantaneous, in the moment phenomena. Everything is one thing on some level. Chemically. Vibrationally. We are all connected. Heavens, do I need to mention 'the butterfly effect'?

What I do to you, I do to me. When I forgive myself, I forgive you. When I forgive you, I forgive myself. When I show you kindness, I show myself kindness.

"The question is the answer." Especially those questions you don't want to ask of yourself and others. Therein lie the most important answers. In Ryan Holiday's book, The Obstacle is the Way, he points out this has been well understood as long as humans have been contemplating our existence and making notes or perhaps pictures about it.

Gabrielle Angel Dee Lilly

The question you most do not want to ask is usually the most direct route to your answer. Take some time to sit in silence and let this settle into you. Let it come out of you. You got this.

The answers are all in you. In the 90's some of us remember a set of cassette tapes --those were little bundles of mylar or some kind of plastic ribbon with data wound around plastic-- Nevermind.

The Silva method on cassette tape was my first introduction to what before that was a purely 'religious suggestion'; that I might imagine myself asking a question to a specific person or to a great library in the 'sky' of my imagination, timeless, not in space, in my mind, and get my answer directly from the Universe, untethered or encumbered by logic. Gestalt communication with the Universe. Some of you might prefer to call this talking to God. Or maybe this is all just a point, talking to a point in the end (Flatland).

Then the internet came along and we kind of got distracted. Lately this has come back around for me. At the same time, more, better, faster. Here we are, finding the right words to ask the question. Aligning with the answers we want to find Making it all happen.

The point is, you don't need to try too hard. Things will come around if you just line up with your good nature. The seed of yin is in the fullest expression of yang. The sprouting seeds of yang are in the emptiest expressions of yin. This just happens. Don't fight it. Ride it. Try to drive it if you like.

Your weakness is your strength. Your strengths are your weaknesses. Sometimes weakness is just weak. That's part of this delightful dance. You get to try things out and see what makes you stronger, and what makes you weaker. Accepting and even embracing our weaknesses makes us stronger, oddly enough. This and many more paradoxes brought to you by 'this crazy life', aka 'la vida loca'.

Cue the Santana portion of the soundtrack. Is there one of those? I think that's actually Ricky Martin.

Many times, our vulnerability is our path to finding our greatness. Most, if not all the authors I admire have personal stories of overcoming fear and weakness and other limiting beliefs to reach new levels of being. Brene Brown, Elizabeth Gilbert, Lewis Howes, Kyle Cease...does he have any weaknesses. Hmmm. JP Sears, Ryan Holiday, David Goggins, Russel Brand—these are all people I consider currently successful, who have unique stories with a similar twist. Transformation. The grind. Showing up and staying in the room (Elizabeth Gilbert, 2015).

Right here and now, by bringing to light some of my own darkest, most vulnerable truths, such as being raped, or abusing flies mindlessly as a child, I feel just a bit more free from shame I didn't even know was pinning me under its shadow. Just like that. Shame and secrecy dissolves, and I am free.

"You have no power over me." (Labyrinth, 1986)

Gabrielle Angel Dee Lilly

It is when we turn around and face those things we fear, that they dissolve into the everything and nothing they came from. So turn around. Face yourself. It won't kill you. Something will eventually, but it probably won't be your vulnerability. It could be your overprotection of it. Give it time.

Be brave. Go lightly; and leap into the unknown which is calling you, even with your weaknesses in hand. You just might be surprised to find they turn out to be the very tools you need in the end.

"Vulnerability is the birthplace of connection and the path to the feeling of worthiness. If it doesn't feel vulnerable, the sharing is probably not constructive." ~Brene' Brown

Gabrielle Angel Dee Lilly

~Angel Lilly, January 2019

truth forty

"Resistance is futile, and necessary."

Star trek demonstrated this nicely with the Borg concept. I suppose the Matrix and Bladerunner and every other science fiction movie produced in my lifetime has ultimately been exploring this question. When to hold, and when to fold (Kenny Rogers crept in there).

In many ways, we are all facing this question, all along the way. Even more now with artificial intelligence knock, knock, knocking at our cellar door. To give in to the masses, or to think for ourselves. To gather masses to our own cause, or to be the lone rogue.

Ah, to be a rebel with a cause.

Is that 'teen spirit' I smell, or something greasier, with less viscosity? Velocity.

Like most things, resistance looks different from different angles. From some positions, it seems like to surrender is to give in, in all the wrong ways, and indeed, it is to give in.

Resistance is not always futile. Sometimes the resistance wins. You gotta feel your way through that one. The urge to resist should be examined a bit, if possible, to determine where it is coming from and what it is resisting against.

Having boundaries to push against sometimes is important, for example, and reestablishing them by bouncing off of them now and then is healthy, I would argue. We could go down the rabbit hole of electrons and insulation and independence, or my mini-trampoline, but let's not, at least, not just now. We can do that in a different book.

The kind of resistance demonstrated against the 'Borg' of Star Trek is the kind of resistance to change we need to contemplate all along the path of conscious evolution. At least, that is a theory I am putting on the table for now.

The more you push against things, the more they push back. And yet, we must resist what we do not want to go willingly towards. To give in without a fight, when we believe strongly in something, is to lose before we begin. Then again, maybe fighting is not the only way.

Always try. Be on the side you think is right. Or walk alone when that seems like the right path for you. You get choose. When to hold, when to give in. When to push back, and when to climb. Don't forget to forgive often. Make time for the things and people and ideas that are most important to you. Stand your ground, but don't waste too much energy putting up a fight when you don't need to. Now and then you might.

When you find yourself pushing against something very hard, remember to be more like water. Be gentle and patient. Find another way. Make a new way. If you push too hard against something, you are liable to become more and more like what you are pushing against. Better to lead, or to go alone, than to use all your energy pushing against a past you don't favor.

Part of that great mystery is not knowing, when exactly we will decide we have had enough. We don't know exactly when or how we will die, we only know we will one day. We don't know when or why we will change our mind and see the other side is right, or when we will triumph in our resistance.

It is the totality of that dance that makes the surface tension which keeps this whole thing movable and flexible. All the delicious, delicate, little steps. Without all that it's just the nothing next to nothing. Quicksand. The muck.

Don't get stuck in the muck.

Relax.

"There is nothing permanent except change."
~Heraclitus (c. 535-475 BCE)

"The most difficult thing in life is to know yourself."
~Thales (c. 624-546 BCE)

Gabrielle Angel Dee Lilly

"Make a Mark"
~Angel Lilly, January 2019

truth forty-one

"How to Be A Peace Warrior"

"Confrontation is a key to good communication." I am a Peace Warrior. As such, I don't want to tell you how to be. I just want to encourage you to be fully yourself, peacefully. And allow that for me. I believe in the value and validity of the ideal and actuality of peaceful conflict resolution. Societally, this is still an ideal, from most perspectives. Individually, it is very much a potential actuality. I know because I can find peaceful conflict resolution in me. I like to wear pink sometimes.

Learning to navigate disagreement and differences of opinion is a cornerstone of society as I like to imagine it. In an ideal society, we can discuss our differences under the umbrella of 'getting along' and the intention of broadening our perspectives, increasing understanding, and finding ways to utilize our diversity and differences to reach common goals.

Gabrielle Angel Dee Lilly

We need to be able to dialogue without being so rigid in our ways that we can't listen to each other. We also need to be certain enough of our opinions that we can articulate our positions, at least sometimes. And we need to be willing to fail. Willing to discover we are wrong or misinformed or unjustly biased, and then, we need to be willing to change our minds. Don't waste your time looking for reasons to be offended. Just take what you think is useful and move along.

From our internal struggles, where we learn to confront our own self-deceit and self-imposed limitations, to our external, societal, even earthly struggles; confrontation of whatever is bothering us is the way to grow through it. Dissolve it. By dealing with whatever is the issue at hand, working it out peacefully and then moving forward, we can stop being stagnant in our relationships with others and with our selves. We can build new, more peaceful, and dynamically interactive, societies on this Earth.

Constructive criticism and feedback is one of the most valuable things we can give each other and ourselves, especially when we are trying to grow. I hope we can learn to share what we think with one another more often. Comparison can be the 'thief of joy' (Bach), or it can be a useful tool to help us decide where we want to be, and which direction we want to move in.

Comparison can motivate us to be better. Examples from those we look up to, or admire, can give us a direction to aim for when we are not clear how to begin. Later, when we notice their fallibility, mortality, 'flaws' and mistakes, they give us permission to be our own imperfect versions of our selves. Today. Here. Now.

Drive forward.

We can 'imitate the masters' when we like the patterns they are creating. We can do it differently, decide to change it up, look and see it a different way, when we disagree. Communication is 'King'. Goddessness.

I mean, communication seems to be the real point of all of it to me. Connections. Articulations. Reflections of ourselves in each other. Shared perspectives with the purpose of expanding awareness. Evolution, baby. Seriously, what is the point of any of it if we don't at least try to communicate?

One of my very favorite things about living, is the seemingly infinite ways we can find and create to communicate. The internet, emojis, sound, color, coming full circle to biomagnetism and DNA. Masculine and feminine. Love. Vibrations. Music. Art. Gestures. Dance. Human expression is one of my all-time super-star favorites of all time.

Did I mention time already? Oh yeah, there it is, time. There is a time factor. Does cinnamon always smell the same to you?

Communication out of context loses its desired effect. Without a 'pin' in time, meaning becomes tangled up, impossible to decipher or agree on. Muddy. Communication takes on so many forms. It is always searching for, and finding, new ways to agree. Maybe that is love.

I learned early-on, the silent communications of touch, and smells, and eyes, and smiles. The nods and the strokes. The leaning in, and the turn away. I grew up in the country with animals, trees, rocks, plants, soils. Worms.

Gabrielle Angel Dee Lilly

I know it all well. I have seen most of the usual moves. The soft love, the sharp love, the envy, the 'you can't have me'. The 'leave me be', the not today, the getaway, the stink, the stank, the sick, the help me please, the please stay with me and keep me warm tonight. My cat friend, Sapphire practices that one on me regularly.

All of these are so easy to understand when they are silent. In 'the animal kingdom', where supposedly consciousness is on a lower dimension. I don't know if I agree with this assessment, and, even if I put 'other animals' on a different part of the spectrum of consciousness and self-awareness from humans, I don't think lower is necessarily the right way to think of it. Maybe it's only lower like F is to G, unless you loop all the way around to the next octave. Anyhow, complex emotions like love are easy to communicate among our fellow animals. Perhaps we humans have more complex feelings, and so need more complex ways of expressing them. Or perhaps our feelings just seem more complex when we express them in more complex ways.

This is also why music will always be one of my favorite ways to communicate. It so smoothly transcends the barriers that words run into on their own. Music transcends hierarchy. It's an equalizer, like love, and silence, and Truth.

By teaming up with rhythm and rhyme, words become something else, in context purely of a song. A place in time and space, outside time and space. Song is one of my favorite methods of communication. Simple and complex songs delight me.

Ah...songs. I have two or three calling to me from the full moon, pulling at my boot laces and heart strings right now. Three. Back to communications though. Where was I? Oh yeah. Outcomes.

It is important to consider what outcomes we want before we communicate. Thinking about the outcomes we want before engaging is an important step in good communications. Effective, maybe is a better word.

If we just want to be heard, or hear ourselves, process out loud, or 'vent', for example, it's good to know that is the outcome we want and communicate that before we start when possible. If collaboration or connection is the goal, then choose those words and cadences that serve that purpose, and approach the scene with the mood you want to be in.

Match the communication style of the person or people or being you are trying to exchange meaning with, from body language to tone and cadence if you can, without seeming like you are mocking them, of course. Keep your vibration high and your mood positive.

Be ready to be ready for what you want to happen.

"Show us what you got." (Rick and Morty)

"The most important thing in communication is hearing what isn't said." ~Peter Drucker

Gabrielle Angel Dee Lilly

"I have several times made a poor choice by avoiding a necessary confrontation." ~John Cleese

"Strong minds discuss ideas, average minds discuss events, weak minds discuss people."
~Socrates (c. 469-399 BCE)

Gabrielle Angel Dee Lilly

"Folding in Unfolding"
~Angel Lilly, January 2019

truth forty-two

"You've got untapped potential, baby."

I was probably about 7 when I first heard The Hitchhiker's Guide to the Galaxy on the radio. My son just delighted me today by mentioning he watched the movie version of it again recently. He and I read it together when he was around 7 too.

When I was 7, there was no internet, and my family did not have a TV. Give me 'second' to feel old. The Hitchhiker's Guide was still just a book and a play. And a radio broadcast series, which was on every Sunday night for a long while. Later it was Moon Over Morocco.

We would all gather in the living-room and listen to the radio play, imagining our own versions of what the streets and the characters looked like. It was maybe the only thing we did as a family back then, or ever, for that matter, except get fire-wood for winter a few times. And pick fruit. And go to church. There were probably other things. The point is none of that.

The point is, this was the first time I heard that the answer to everything is 42. At that time, it didn't exactly make much sense, but it sat well with me, especially in the context of that book, and in its own way, it did make perfect sense.

As I look back at it now, I can see how part of the brilliance of that book series, is how the truth permeates things, no matter what we do. The truth seeps through, even if the words are ridiculous. Even if the likelihood and correctness of any of it is delightfully improbable. Like most of the best things in life, it doesn't quite seem to make sense. And yet it does. This is a perfect answer to everything. 42.

"Why? Because." That's a song (Happiness Runs, Donovan). That one reminds me of that Over the Rainbow rendition by that one Hawaiian guy. You know the one.

Somewhere over the Rainbow - Israel "IZ" Kamakawiwoʻole.

That one almost always brings tears to my eyes. I think he had a lot of untapped potential, and also, tapped into a great deal of it, by being true to his own nature. I'm guessing you and I do too.

Your way is the best way. Only you can know what that is. You will know by how it feels. It can get better and better, or worse. You almost always get to decide, remember? Maybe even always. What is your favorite part of the color wheel today?

How much, and what, do you want to be? I know, it's a lot of responsibility sometimes, which is why you shouldn't overthink it. Don't overthink it. Feel your way into it and through it. Follow what feels good to you. Not the sulking, hurt, armored, little kid you. The true, realized, waking you. Just trust that you have your own back, and that maybe the Universe knows things you don't.

For all your own yet undiscovered potential, there is infinitely more untapped potential just lying around, untapped, in every nook and cranny, every vast empty space, every worm-hole to infinity, so the odds really are in your favor that everything good will happen to you. You just gotta' give it some time.

None of that is really the point either. Not exactly. It's that infinitely untapped part, the potential, that you can tap into. I know, the words get in the way (cue the music).

Get ready to be ready to receive what you are ready for.

There are some really exiting discoveries going on right now, in our own evolution. In creating a global culture. In artificial intelligence. In space travel. In the microbiome, nanotechnology, psychology and brain science.

The fields that excite me the most when I think about our future are architecture, education, mind science, music, healing, soil and forest reclamation, and community building. Making new connections on large and small scales. Building bridges. Fortifying old ones. Tearing down obsolete ones. Our work is never done. Best make it fun!

Send in the clowns?

Gabrielle Angel Dee Lilly

*"Think big and don't listen to people who tell you it
can't be done. Life's too short to think small."*
~Tim Ferriss

"Your past is not your potential. In any hour you can choose to liberate the future."
~Marilyn Ferguson

Gabrielle Angel Dee Lilly

"Smooth and Spiny"
~Angel Lilly, December 2018

truth forty-three

"Things come in waves."

There are natural cycles to things. It's important not to get bogged down in the down cycles. That's life, baby. The way the cookie crumbles sometimes. Catch it on the upswing.

If you look around, it is impossible to miss the repeating patterns and cycles all around and in you. The earth has cycles, which bring us the seasons. The sun has cycles, which we translate into eons. Your body has cycles. Life has cycles. Weather has cycles. There are sexual cycles, relationship cycles, business cycles, water cycles, life cycles, societal cycles, historical cycles. Bicycles. Motorcycles… Cycles of peace and war. You can find patterns in anything you look at.

Even chaos has its cyclical nature. The way yin contains the seed of yang and yang contains the seed of yin, so too does chaos contain order, and order contain chaos. Things turn into their opposite, and then back again. That is the pendulum swing of resistance-based living. Of course, there are infinitely potential other ways. I like the idea of less resistance, more flowing-river based living, the further out from shore I get.

You can learn to recognize the patterns of cycles in your own body, and in the rest of nature. Avoid struggling against your own nature. Avoid struggling against any nature if you can, unless you are using it to push against and propel yourself forward.

Better yet, you can learn to ride those waves, baby. The art of surfing, snowboarding, being a good lover, parent, teacher, student, leader; what you will get out of any of it depends on how well you learn to read, understand, comprehend, anticipate, and utilize natural cycles.

Maybe we can learn to write in them? Is the next phase an awakening and integration of what we currently call the subconscious? Will we learn to navigate the waves of potential we currently see as 'too far out', and then swim towards the next and the next and the next ones? I think probably there is a good chance of that. I think we can learn to grab the mane and tail of some other-worldly dragon energy and become the wave. The main and tale? This is what I feel I am doing here right now, right here.

Patterns are your friends when you know how to use them. Time your approach. Hold on. Paddle fast. Pop up. Ride. Repeat. This is the best way to live a life if you ask me.

Some people seem content to just bob around in the sea, letting the current take them as it pleases. That is a fine way to be too, just not for me.

Not yet at least. Not today. I love to cooperate with creation as we create me. I love that I get so much choice in sensation, color, and flavor combinations. It's important to try new things now and then.

Daily habits and seasonal rituals are the cornerstones, the framework, for putting good patterns in place. Like the windowsills we put our pies on. A quick examination of your daily habits and seasonal rituals will tell you if you are aiming for the high points of the waves or if you have been struggling for the troughs. The choice is always each of ours.

Wash those windows now and then. Paint the sills.

Some people seem to struggle so hard, seem to work at catching every low part. They work harder than those that ride the waves if you ask me. They never catch a break. They get the shit end of the stick every time.

If this sounds anything like your story, I strongly advise you to consider upgrading your story immediately. Start today. Catch a train...or a wave.

Gabrielle Angel Dee Lilly

"It's not what you've got, it's what you use that
makes a difference."
~Zig Ziglar

"Beauty Repeats Itself:
~Angel Lilly, November 2018

Gabrielle Angel Dee Lilly

truth forty-four

"Repetition Works"

I repeat. Repetition. It works.

Get it? Great. Go on then. Get some on ya'.

Repetition is how the patterns get in. How we learn what the words are. For better and for worse. It works. Say it one more time with me for good measure. All together now. "Repetition works." See? You will remember that, at least for a little while. And if I get you to say it a few more times with me... Ready? "Repetition Works!", and better yet, repeat it in different ways so that you understand it better and better each time. "Repetition what?" Works, silly.

If I can say, or show it just a little different, and still the same thing...like...telling the same story a hundred million bajillion trillion different ways...the same freaking story. I digress. Where was I? Oh yeah. The inner workings of repetition.

Seriously though, repetition is what establishes patterns, Patterns are anything you notice or worth making a word about, so, it's pretty important if you want to make a point or leave a 'mark' of any sort. They say to be a Legacy, your work or name or idea must outlive you by at least 100 years. Is that what they say? Or did one person say it?

Well, first, one person says it...

What is the 'mark' you want to leave on this world while you are here, and after you are gone? For how long?

It's the first follower who makes the leader into a leader and not just a crazy lunatic, on the fringe. I guess that is how to start a new pattern or make a drastic change in an existing one. I can't tell you anything you don't already know, though, even if I find a new way to put it into words. Even if I write a new song about it. We each get to choose, based on our own best guesses of what is best, when to lead and when to follow. Where to go and how to go there.

What I am really trying to get at here, is the way the Universe seems to be constant iterations, reiterations, repetitions of itself, and that evolution seems to be what happens through the minute changes that happen through these iterations. And that it is our freedom to choose, freewill, if you will, which creates those delightful little changes, opens the doors of possibility to new things. It's up to each of us—up to me and to you—to decide how much we want to try to copy and how much we want to try to change, and how we will imbed the new in the old.

Since I get to choose what I repeat the most, I choose gratitude, generosity, and joy. This is the part where what you choose becomes what you get, what chooses you. Choose wisely, what you will repeat. Practicing feelings and expressions of gratitude and generosity are a pretty sure way to cultivate lots of joy in your life and in the lives of those around you.

Gabrielle Angel Dee Lilly

Finding new ways to express gratitude and expressing gratitude for the things I have, and the things I know are coming to me, is an excellent way to increase the odds of their arrival. It also increases the odds they will stick around longer and cultivate and revel in more joy and playfulness. Along with playfulness and creativity, I aim to

Gratitude, graciousness, gentleness, and generosity add up to greatness in my geometry.

Life is just iterations of itself, trying, unfolding, blooming, dying. New combinations of fragrances and colors. Something next to another thing. Sometimes you get the pure, permeating, darkly light sweetness of vanilla. Why not choose the things that make you feel most whole, most alive, and most on purpose? Only you can know exactly what that is for you. Not the hurt dead and dying you, unless that is the 'you' you really want to be. I prefer the strong, kind, alive and shining brightly right now you.

Bloom.

Will you come with me. or are you going your own way?

Whether you try to copy it exactly, or you set about to make something completely original, you will still be just another iteration of you and your kind. Have at it. You really can't get it wrong if you take a broad enough perspective. We are destined to repeat and destined to vary. It's our nature, or at least, it sure seems that way to me. Let me know if you disagree.

"We are what we repeatedly do. Excellence, then, is not an act, but a habit."
~Aristotle (c. 384-322 BCE)

Gabrielle Angel Dee Lilly

"Our Hearts Fly"
~Angel Lilly, January 2019

"Find the place inside yourself where nothing is impossible." ~Deepak Chopra

truth forty-five

"The only answer is yes."

You can pout and miss out, or you can get what you get and like it. Or, you can take charge, change, and build a life you love!

Building a life on 'yes' rather than 'no', is really the only way to go. Because of a tricky clause in the fine print somewhere behind the curtain of the 'law of attraction', focusing on what you don't want, only gets you more of it. The only way to get what you do want more of is to focus on that. And not on the lack of it, on what you already have of it. You've got to find it first in yourself, know what it feels like to have it already, and be grateful for that. See? There.

We cast our votes for our collective future reality by way of what we focus on, how we respond to what we feel, the choices we make.

Do you like honey in your tea?

The Universe does not pay any mind to your words. Words are not the things they point to. It only pays attention to what the words are pointing to. The feelings. The vibrations. The alignment.

What's behind your words?

This means, the word "no", is meaningless in the grand design. Anytime you say "no", really you are in effect, saying yes to it, by way of focusing on it. Therefore, it's best not to confuse yourself or the Universe, and just find the things you want to say "yes" to and keep doing that. More of that.

K.I.S.S. "Keep it simple, silly.

I want to say a little more about cultivating lower vibrations; victims and victimizers. Victims and the people that victimize them are on two different ends of the same vibrational stick.

Don't get your 'panties in a wad'. Your socks all bunched up? I'm not trying to get into a debate about whether 'no means no' with regards to our sexuality, though again, that may be another book. I do welcome any dialogue you would like to have with me about that.

I am saying, the abused become abusers. It's a cycle. It has a pattern. You can break out of it, once you see it and accept it. Love it, even. I understand that is a leap you might not be ready for. Just hold a tiny space for the possibility that everything is going to work out okay; okay?

I know we can evolve beyond the cycle of abused and abuser because I have been in it. And I am evolving from it.

When you approach every sentence you speak, with the idea of speaking into existence what you do want, then you will be a master of deliberate design.

Gabrielle Angel Dee Lilly

That sounds and looks good on paper. I have yet to master it, so I cannot actually attest that this is a certain truth. It's more of a working theory in practice. Something I am working on, really. When I am able to use positively rooted, 'yes-based' words to communicate, it is amazing how quickly the positive opportunities escalate in my life.

Perhaps the question is just, how much, and when, and what will I be ready for?

Dive in.

"Play to Love, Love to Play"
~Angel Lilly, January 2019

truth forty-six

"Love is the answer."

I am not always sure that this is always true. I do think it is the best answer though. Truly.

There does seem to be some universal truth to the vibrational aspects of love. Every animal I have ever gotten to know, seems to understand some version of it. The cells of my body seem to respond to it. There is some evidence that water responds to it. Certainly, water, sand, air, and everything, does respond to vibrations in general. Different musical notes produce different patterns in water and in sand, for example.

I'm curious now about minerals. I wonder if they speak a language we might call love. Isn't a crystal in some ways, love? What about the sun? Maybe. Not really. Depends on how you spell it out, I guess. Semantics, that.

Since I am a complex tapestry of minerals, woven together, even becoming this worn, familiar song full of all the rich things we say go into a love song...I have to wonder.

"Stop. With your feet in the air and your head on the ground, try this trick and spin it" That's the Pixies, Where is My Mind. I sing this song in a cover band I am in. Covers are alright by me. Though they didn't used to be.

Do you think stars and planets and moons 'fall' in love? Are they sometimes so overcome with attraction for another that they will risk the certain present for an exciting unknown potential future? Is love an attraction?

To me, love is an enigma. Like you. Like me.

Love is my favorite part of the Great Mystery.

We have a lot of different meanings attached to love. Like snow, it comes in many textures, speeds, shades, temperatures... Every flake is unique.

Just because you love something or someone else today, does not reduce the amount or legitimacy of what you loved before. We seem to feel that it is disrespectful to the one we love now to still love the ones we have loved, or disrespectful to the ones we have loved to love someone new. So silly, that.

I've learned a lot from snowboarding over the last 7-8 years. One of the greatest lessons has been that, in order to really enjoy what you love, you have to let go of expectations, and be prepared to navigate whatever terrain and conditions come at you with a positive attitude.

If you start to get tired or grumpy, take a break!

Gabrielle Angel Dee Lilly

"What would love do?"
~Dr. Joe Dispenza

You can hurt yourself snowboarding if you continue when you are no longer doing it with love. Same with love, if you aren't doing it with snowboarding. No, wait. That probably isn't true for most of you. I meant to say, in order to enjoy the complex, dynamic, ever changing and not completely in your control fun-ride we sometimes call love, you gotta' let go of expectations. Holding on too tightly can hurt.

Be prepared for any conditions. Have good skills to navigate whatever comes with a positive attitude. If you find yourself getting grumpy, take a break. Eat a snack. Take a walk. Have a bath. Get a massage. Do whatever you need to, in order to stay in the game, and to show up 'on the court' ready to play. *Did I just go sports arena Athena on mybadself?*

Be the love. Bring the love. Don't skimp on the love sauce. Everything is better with more love...Exceptn' maybe killin'. ... .. Nope. Even that.

Love is part of The Great Mystery. It may not be the Universal language. Then again, it just might be. Perhaps we just need to practice learning different ways of speaking it to really see?

Ironically beautiful, wouldn't it be, if the truest truth turned out to be the greatest mystery?

Hold on! Hold on. Did you just go from love to snowboarding to basketball to killing in one paragraph? Did I, I mean. We. Well, no. Now it's two or three. Or four. Yeah... Okay. Just checkin'.

Here's a thing I'll say about 'real love'. True love. Not bondage or codependence or attachment or obsession. The unconditional, foundational love that seems to be at the heart of everything. Real love must always have choice.

'Must' might be a bit rigid.

Love is weakened by insecure ego identities and narrow thinking. Real love is steeped in freedom. In mystery and security in the unknown. In fluid choices. In dualities and individualities. Expansion. True love invites us to choose pleasure. Choose joy. Choose to give and receive. To share appreciation, support, and perspectives. And it offers contrast. Less pleasant aspects we can learn from.

Love frequently gets complicated by relationships. Social and familiar contracts. Attractions and repulsions. Hormones and pheromones. Cultural norms and individual biases. So many details filter the ways we allow ourselves to explore love. This can be beautiful and painful. It is often both. I love that. There is room for endless diversity in love, just as there is in music, and in life.

Gabrielle Angel Dee Lilly

"True love stories never have endings."
~Richard Bach

"Your Heart Knows My Heart"
~Angel Lilly, January 2019

Gabrielle Angel Dee Lilly

My heart is not empty for the ones I miss.

I do not feel so much the abyss, as the full bellied laughter languished only by loving someone so deeply, so truly, so flawliciously as this.
~GAL

"There are forces in nature called Love and Hate. The force of Love causes elements to be attracted to each other and to be built up into some particular form or person, and the force of Hate causes the decomposition of things."
~Empedocles (c. 490-330 BCE)

truth forty-seven

"This too shall pass."

You're gonna' die. So am I. We might live more fully alive if we kept this more fully in mind more of the time.

It's all transitory. Everything is temporary. Like a dream.

Don't worry, be happy. Make time to enjoy the fragrance of your peppermint tea. Soak in the blueness of the sky.

If you have a better plan than happiness, or any plan you think might be worth trying out, please share it. I really would love to hear it. This is how we build the future. If you take away nothing else from this book, please take away knowing that it is my dream to help build connections, facilitate healings, unity, and bring out whatever you consider to be the greatness in you.

Everything good and bad, everything you enjoy and don't enjoy; you, me, the oceans and the trees. It is all just tiny shiny specks of Universe, sparkling in the breeze.

If you could build-your-own Super Hero or Super Villian, what would your Super Powers be?

Everything dissolves and disappears eventually. I think it is important to remember that, and not waste much time dwelling on the past, or on the unknown future. Step fully into the right now and here. Be fully in the present, and then see how you want to feel. Get what you get and like it, or pout and miss out. The choice is yours. At least it seems to be, to me.

Don't fret over the parts that are not your favorite. Grit your teeth, grin, and bear it, or learn to look at it another different way. Ideally, you can learn to find ways to see things differently, or change them, if they really are unpleasant to you.

In any case, don't worry. It will be over soon. Worrying seems like one of the very least enjoyable or productive things we do. I am sure there is a healthy dosage for that too.

This is a good place to tell you the "Big Rocks First' story. It's to remind you to take care of the most important things in your life first. Then fill in the rest. Your time and space are finite, even if the Universe is not.

I took a qi gong seminar some years ago, from a ninjutsu master. He has a ninjutsu school in Boston, the only one of its kind. He studied under grand master flash--I mean, The Grand Master, Masaaki Hatsumi.

The man teaching this seminar had produced more than a dozen instructional videos and published several well-selling books. He ran his school, and toured around the US sometimes, speaking at events, and teaching seminars such as the one I was attending.

Gabrielle Angel Dee Lilly

The seminar was great, and still benefits me today, a decade or so later. It still smells of sweat and Nag Champa in my mind.

The man teaching this seminar said he practiced meditation, five-element breathing, and iron-shirt for three hours or more on most days. All the while smiling, and mindful of his posture and energy. Someone in the class asked him how on earth he found time to do that while traveling and doing so many other things.

He told us about a professor of his, who, for class one day, filled a glass jar with large stones and asked his students if the jar was full. Most of them said yes. The professor then put in some smaller marbles, in between the stones.

Again, he asked the students "Is the jar full now?" Some of them said yes. The professor then poured sand into the jar, and again, asked them if it was full. Again, most of the students said yes. Then the professor filled the jar with water. I guess we should consider it full there, though there is probably infinitely more we could put in there if you really put your imagination to it…water filled with intentions, and love, music even. Perhaps the fragrance of pine trees.

The point of that story is, 'put the big rocks in first'. My mom just brought that story up at lunch today, telling me she's thought of it a few times and it has helped her. I love that.

What the big rocks are, you get to decide.

Your jar will fill up before you know it. It's your space. It's your time. It's this life. And it is finite, at least, it seems to be from here.

You will die, most likely too soon. Make the most of the time you have. Savor the flavors and enjoy the rides. Let go of what does not serve you or delight you or a least, tickle your 'fancy'. Cultivate creativity and curiosity into your truth.

Keep the music alive.

Gabrielle Angel Dee Lilly

"Flypta"
~Angel Lilly, January 2019

"The mark of your ignorance is the depth of your belief in injustice and tragedy. What the caterpillar calls the end of the world, the Master calls the butterfly." Richard Bach

Gabrielle Angel Dee Lilly

"Unicorn on rug in moonlight"
~Angel Lilly, January 2019

"Unicorn looks in my window"
~Angel Lilly, January 2019

Conclusions:

Before you go, I would like to repackage these three truths for you to take with you. Consider this a gift, from me to you.

1. People are basically, mostly good. Even if they aren't, be nice. Trapped animals can be dangerous. Anyone being 'not nice' is most likely feeling trapped. Even you. So be kind. Especially to yourself. Forgive often. Move along now.

2. Your body is the only thing you really can't live this life without. Take good care of it and it will carry you far. Neglect it and you will pay with your life. Simple as. The degree to which we learn to live fully integrated, in our bodies, is the degree to which we truly live alive. Train your body, including your brain. Don't be a slave to your body's past addictions.

3. Timing matters, dosage matters, state matters, people matter, you matter. In this physical world, everything is matter. Waves move matter, and you can be the wave. It's the nothing that makes up the matter. Silence makes the music. Everything and nothing maters. Both. Potential is greater than probability.

     People need to be ready, or nearly ready, in order to receive a new idea or change underlying beliefs. I believe we are in the midst of a great paradigm shift. I hold space for the possibility we will evolve into a more connected and more beautifully individual collection of beings.

As we co-create this collective, ever evolving story, I have genuine, high hopes that we will create new common languages, or new ways of understanding our old languages.

"Relax, nothing is under control."

Ready or not, here I come.

Gabrielle Angel Dee Lilly

"My Black Stone Heart Warms In The Sun"
~Angel Lilly

47 truths

Gabrielle Angel Dee Lilly

Bonus tracks?

Let's talk about sex, baby.
Where there is a will, there is a way.
Privileges and obligations.
Invent your way.
Where there is a will there is a way.
K.I.S.S. Keep it simple, silly.
Forgiveness.
Ego trains.
Transcendence.
Global economies.
Gratitude.
Generosity.
Reciprocity.
Appreciation.
Grace.

Coming soon to a conversation near you.

"Don't believe what your eyes are telling you. All they show is limitation. Look with your understanding, find out what you already know, and you'll see the way to fly."
~Richard Bach

47 truths

Gabrielle Angel Dee Lilly

"Tyrannabird"
~Angel Lilly, January 2019

About Me:

I am a Modern-Day Multi-Medium Storyteller.

My personal pursuit for truth has many facets, of course. Like I imagine everyone's does.

In the last two decades my studies have mostly been filtered through, and swayed towards, the intentions around evolutionary leadership, paradigm shifting, mindfulness, self-awareness, comedy, music, ceramics, large-scale construction, gardening, photography, and education. These are the tools I have to work with, and the lenses I tend to see things through.

I dropped out of high-school after skipping ahead a couple grades. Then I went to college for a very long time. About 15 years. I have a few degrees and a lot of certificates. I have loved. I have lost. I am a mom, a daughter, and a friend. I've been a self-employed artist, a student, a visionary leader, and freelancer most of my life. My studies and experiences cluster in the sciences, arts, natural healing, storytelling, patterns, business, education, music, poetry, trees, architecture, and clay. Oh, yeah, and cement.

Epilogue:

Why am I writing, or why did I write this book? If you didn't ask, I still will. I really want to know.

In part, this book is a personal exploration of what I believe, an attempt to uncover and untangle those gold and silver and green threads holding everything together, deep at my core. Like so many before me, I am compelled sometimes to hunt down the most beautiful truths and pin them down like those special butterflies and occasional moths we used to collect in elementary school, and maybe again later in college.

Why do we like butterflies so much more than moths?

Truth be told, I would much rather leave them flying freely, flapping their own colorful wings for as long as their nature allows. Moths and butterflies and truths. I don't like pinning things down until they are dead. I don't like to be pinned down very much myself.

I just want to stir things up a little. Ask some questions. Clarify what's what and who is who in this story. Find the 'big whys' (Simon Sinek). Explore the infinite potential 'how's.

And how.

I'd like to make the truth fly a bit. Inhale some of it. Like running through a mountain meadow of wildflowers, along the banks of a cool stream, stirring up butterflies and dragonflies. I just want to giggle at their silliness and marvel at their diverse, simple beauty. Watch them glisten in the sun.

Maybe there is something important here, or near. I do feel it is a good time for us to communicate more freely, more openly, more honestly, more lovingly. Perhaps we can dance together a little more? Smile more? Let go of our differences and find more common ground to build our beautiful futures on? I hope so.

Truths are a lot like butterflies and moths and bees and trees to me. Kittens and puppies. Worms and dust bunnies. I would like to spend a little more time getting to know them all a little better.

Since I am sure by now that you are a truth seeker and at least, some kind of reality dancer, like me; I cordially invite you to share more of your own truths with me. As I figure out my own working truths, I'll tell you what I have figured out of mine so far, or at least, I will attempt to. This is what I am hoping to do here.

I am 47 this year. That is not any kind of a record or anything. It is kind of a misleading label though. It seems like it should mean something, when actually it means very little. Nothing really, as far as I can tell. It's just this number we keep track of. Our age.

Gabrielle Angel Dee Lilly

I met a woman this year who lives in a culture that does not write down or remember birthdates. In the Middle East somewhere. She chooses whatever day she likes to celebrate her birthday each year. She figures she's 70. October 8th was a good day to make your birthday this year, she told me. It happened to be a few days after that.

Labels are mostly not my favorite, although I do like numbers a lot. They are related to music in some mysterious or obvious way.

I celebrated my 47th birthday last January, on the 25th. Celebrated might be an exaggeration too, though maybe not. I honestly can't remember. As I write this intro, the big 48 looms in the not very distant future. Anyhow, 47. That is a lot of "7s".

I like to say that, mostly because it doesn't really make sense and yet, somehow still does. To me. I like 7's, and multiples of 7's. I like 11's too. Mostly because they rhyme with 7's. And because of the way they add up to two. And 3's...

Just one of a bunch of little facts about me you will probably never need to know. These are the little things that delight me in life. That is a pretty good reason right there and all the credentials I need to write a book like this, really.

...but wait, there's more!

In many ways this is closing the loop on a project I started when I was about 12 I think. Or maybe I was 14. Sometimes after my grandmother died.

I think I called it "A Metalist's Handbook" or something like that. A friend of mine's older brother had just introduced me to weed and Black Sabbath. Sweet Leaf. In a van, of course.

Everyone lived by the river back then. In houses, mostly.

I remember thinking I was rewriting my own version of the bible, after realizing the whole church thing was a sham-just a congregation hand-groomed by a select few to give them first access to the minds and bodies of young girls and boys as they grew up. Looking back, it is easy to see a path from there to here. Looking forward it is not always so easy to see so clearly.

Anyhow, I suppose it's also merely 'an age thing'. Many people around my age begin to pontificate and reflect on our stories and epiphanies. Time to write version one of my memoirs. Or is this version three. I can't remember. Or I am not sure. Whichever suits you better.

In part, I suppose this book is an attempt of sorts to communicate with my son across the ages. Maybe my father too, I don't know. Probably some other people I love as well.

It might be a bit of an obligation for me as well. That baby elephant in the corner over there might say my particular privileged white American Girl position puts me peculiarly in place to pose presently here. Like some pie. Exactly like.

Mostly, it is an exploration. Like all good adventures, I don't know exactly how it will end or what twists and turns will reveal themselves to me as I make my idea into an actual book. I can tell you, these truths have been simmering a long time in the pot that is my mind.

Gabrielle Angel Dee Lilly

This is your invitation to dance in the potential meanings of truth, love, life, happiness, communication, and liberty with me. Do you smell cardamom? Is that cinnamon? Peaches?

It is also the foundation for very many great things to come in my life, and in life in general I feel. As we navigate our collective futures, writing this book just feels right, feels very much in alignment with everywhere I have been and everywhere I am going. It's closing a delightfully dizzying number of loops for me, in my story.

I am excited to share it with you and I am excited to see where it takes me. Already, in putting all this down on paper, and preparing to share it publicly, I get a little –Ooo --was that a butterfly? Dare I say it kind of gives me butterflies in my stomach?

That really does make me laugh out loud.

Butterfly analogies are everywhere.

They get kind of pesky after a while, don't they?

Like anything.

"ODeeYay", by Angel Lilly, 2019

Gabrielle Angel Dee Lilly

"This is not a time in history to know, this is a time in history to know how."
~Dr. Joe Dispenza (2018)

Roll Credits:

Mentions and Influences/References:

The Alphabet Versus the Goddess, The Conflict Between Word and Image, By: Leonard Shlain, Viking Press, 1998.

A Rickle in Time, Rick and Morty,Episode, Season 2 Episode 1, Directed by Wes Archer, Written by Matt Roller, July 26, 2015.

The Art of Conflict Management: Achieving Solutions for Life, Work, and Beyond, By: Michael Dues, The Great Courses, Audiobook Release date: 2013.

The Art of Not Giving a Fuck: A Counterintuitive Approach To Living A Good Life, by Mark Manson, First Harper One/HarperCollins, 2016.

Big Fish: A Novel of Mythic Proportions, Daniel Wallace, Recorded Books, April 15, 2011.

Blitzscaling: The Lightning-Fast Path to Building Massively Valuable Companies, by Reid Hoffman (Author), Chris Yeh (Author), Bill Gates (Foreword),

The Butter Battle Book: (New York Times Notable Book of the Year) (Classic Seuss)Jan 12, 1984.

Crushing It!: How Great Entrepreneurs Build Their Business and Influence-and How You Can, Too, by Gary Vaynerchuk, 01/30/2018.

Dare to Lead: Brave Work. Tough Conversations. Whole Hearts, Brené Brown, Audible Audiobook, Random House Audio, October 2018.

Disrupt You!: Master Personal Transformation, Seize Opportunity, and Thrive in the Era of Endless Innovation by Jay Samit, July 7, 2015.

Dream Teams, Shane Snow, Penguin Audio, June 5, 2018.

"Dr Joe Dispenza | Becoming Supernatural", YouTube Video, 1:36:47, published by "Dr. Joe Dispenza Videos", December 8, 2018, https://www.youtube.com/watch?v=r3pmEl4Rt_k

"Dr Joe Dispenza | You Are the Placebo - How to exercise the power of mind", YouTube Video, 1:55:48, published by "Dr. Joe Dispenza Videos", Oct 25, 2018, https://www.youtube.com/watch?v=0Uw0hJxy7Y4

The Existential Pleasures of Engineering, by Samuel C. Florman, St. Maritin's Press, 1976.

Flatland: A Romance of Many Dimensions, by Edwin A. Abbott, Dover Publiscations, 1884.

Forest Gump, Director Robert Zemeckis Starring Tom Hanks, Robin Wright Penn, Gary Sinise, 1994.

The Four Noble Truths of Love: Buddhist Wisdom for Modern Relationships, Susan Piver, Lionheart Press, June 1, 2018.

Grapho-therapeutics: The pen and pencil therapy, by Paul de Sainte Columbe, , Popular Library Edition, 1972.
The Hitchhiker's Guide to the Galaxy, by Douglas Adams, Serious Production Books Ltd., 1979.

Habits of Highly Productive People, Brandon Bruchard, Hay House Inc. September 19, 2017.

The Handmaid's Tale, Atwood, Margaret, New York: Anchor Books, a division of Penguin Random House LLC, 1998.

How to Be a Bawse, A Guide to Conquering Life, By: Lilly Singh, Random House Audio, March 28, 2017.

Illusions: The Adventures if a Reluctant Messiah, by Richard Bach, 1977.

Imagine It Forward: Courage, Creativity, and the Power of Change, by Beth Comstock and Tahl Raz, Sep 18, 2018.

Impact Theory, https://impacttheory.com/

James and the Giant Peach, Tim Burton film*, Directed by Henry Selick, Starring Susan Sarandon, Paul Terry, Richard Dreyfuss, 1996.

John Cleese Explores the Health Benefits of Laughter in Comedy, Health, Psychology | April 29th, 2015.

Labyrinth, Staring Jennifer Connelly and David Bowie, Directed by Jim Henson, Screenplay by Terry Jones, 1986.
The 50th Law/The Laws of Human Nature, 50 Cent & Robert Greene, Profile Books, July 9, 2010.

Gabrielle Angel Dee Lilly

The Leader of the Future: New Visions, Strategies, and Practices for the Next Era; Edited by Hesselbein, Goldsmith, and Beckhard, Forward by Peter Drucker, The Drucker Foundation, 1996.

Lewis Howes, The School of Greatness, 2013-current https://www.youtube.com/user/lewishowes

Men in Black II, film starring Tommy Lee Jones and Will Smith, Directed by Barry Sonnenfeld and written by Lowell Cunningham and Robert Gordon, 2002.

Never Split the Difference, Negotiating as if Your Life Depended on It, By: Chris Voss with Tahl Raz, HarperBusiness, May 17th 2016.

The Obstacle Is the Way: The Timeless Art of Turning Trials into Triumph, by Ryan Holiday, Tim Ferriss (Publisher), May 6, 2014.

Out of My Mind, Alan Arkin, Unabridged Audible Audiobook, 12-06-18.

The Power of Vulnerability, Teachings of Authenticity, Connection, and Courage, By: Brené Brown PhD, Sounds True, May 24, 2013.

Pursuit of Truth by W. V. Quine and Steven Crossley, University Press Audiobooks, Nov 21, 2011.

Reclaiming Conversation, Sherry Turkle, Penguin Books, Reprint October 4, 2016.

"Rupert Sheldrake - Is The Sun Conscious?", Recorded at Reconnect 2018, 7th July, Bath UK, Electric Universe UK

Published on Nov 8, 2018,
https://www.youtube.com/watch?v=SFhsObpja8A

The Silva Mind Control Method for Getting Help from Your Other Side. by Jose Silva (Author), Robert B. Stone November, 1989.

"Simon Sinek: How great leaders inspire action" | Video on TED.com, TED Ideas Worth Spreading. Retrieved at October 3, 2011,
https://www.ted.com/talks/simon_sinek_how_great_lead ers_inspire_action?language=en

Start with Why: How Great Leaders Inspire Everyone to Take Action, by Simon Sinek, 2009.

Stealing Fire: How Silicon Valley, the Navy SEALs, and Maverick Scientists Are Revolutionizing the Way We Live and Work, by Steven Kotler & Jamie Wheal, Dey Street Books, May 8, 2018.

The Third Door: The Wild Quest to Uncover How the World's Most Successful People Launched Their Careers, by Alex Banayan, Random House Audio, June 2018.

Unsafe Thinking: How to Be Nimble and Bold When You Need It Most, Jonah Sachs, Hachette Audio, May 11, 2018.

Vivid Vision: A Remarkable Tool For Aligning Your Business Around a Shared Vision of the Future, by Cameron Herold, Lioncrest Publishing, March 19, 2018.

"Your Elusive Creative Genius", Ted talk by Elizabeth Gilbert, TED2009,
https://www.ted.com/talks/elizabeth_gilbert_on_genius?l anguage=en

Gabrielle Angel Dee Lilly

Your One Word: The Powerful Secret to Creating a Business and Life That Matter, by Evan Carmichael, Penguin Audio, 2016.

This Trick Makes You Immune To Illness | Wim Hof on Impact Theory

Dr. Drew on Why Disgust Is the Best Motivation | Impact Theory, Tom Bilyeu, Published on May 16, 2017, https://www.youtube.com/watch?v=fHkGv1HqJYI

A wise man knows nothing.

Gabrielle Angel Dee Lilly

"Sunsets and Moonrises"
by Angel Lilly, December 2018

Suggested Reading and Watch List:

3 Billion Under 30: How Millennials Continue Redefining Success, Breaking Barriers, and Changing The World: 75 Stories of Entrepreneurship, Change, and Leadership, Jared Kleinert, 3 Billion Under 30 LLC, February 26, 2017.

A Coming Of Wizards: A Manual of Human Potential, by Michael E. Reynolds, Solar Survival Press, 1989.

Advice on Dying and Living a Better Life, by the Dalai Lama, translated and edited by Jeffrey Hopkins, Ph.D., Atria Books, 2002.

Big Fish. Director: Tim Burton, Screenplay: John August, Story by: Daniel Wallace, December 25, 2003.

"Eckhart Tolle Laughter Breaks Through the Ego", published on YouTube by Namaste Publishing, Published on Mar 8, 2016.

Everybody Lies: Big Data, New Data, and What the Internet Can Tell Us About Who We Really Are, by Seth Stephens-Davidowitz, February 20, 2018.

I Am a Strange Loop, by Douglas R. Hofstadter, Greg Baglia and Hachette Audio, Sep 24, 2018.

Infinite Possibilities: The Art of Living Your Dreams, Mike Dooley, tut Enterprises, Atria Books/Beyond Words; Reprint edition, September 7, 2010.

James and the Giant Peach, Directed by Henry Selick, Starring Susan Sarandon, Paul Terry, Richard Dreyfuss, 1996.

Last Chance to See, by Douglas Adams and Mark Carwardine, Harmony Books and Serious Productions Ltd., 1990.

Leveraging the Universe and Engaging the Magic, by Mike Dooley, Totally Unique Thoughts, May 1, 2004.
Life's Golden Ticket: A Story About Second Chances, by Brendon Burchard, Harper One, 2008.

Life's Golden Ticket: A Story About Second Chances, by Brendon Burchard, Harper One, 2008.

Love Let Go: Radical Generosity for the Real World, Laura Truax, Amalya Campbell, Jessica Schell, Wm. B. Eerdmans Publishing Company, Audible Audiobook, May 17, 2017.

Love Medicine, by Luise Erdrich, First Harper Perennial, 1984,1993.

Mindset: The New Psychology of Success, by Carol S. Dweck, Ballantine Books, December 26, 2007.

MouseSoup, by Arnold Lobel, Scholastic Books, 1977.

Prescriptions for happiness, ken keyes jr.. Living Love Publications, no publishing date, free to reiterate
Primal Leadership, Realizing the Power of Emotional Intelligence, By: Daniel Goleman, Richard Boyatzis, Annie McKee, Macmillan Audiobook, Audible.com Release Date: May 17, 2002.

Principles: Life and Work, by Ray Dalio, Simon & Schuster, September 19, 2017.

Reclaiming Conversation: The Power of Talk in a Digital Age, Sherry Turkle, Penguin Books, October 6, 2015.

She Had Some Horses, by Joy Harjo, Thunder Mouth Press, 1983.

She Reads Truth: Holding Tight to Permanent in a World That's Passing Away, Raechel Myers, Amanda Bible, Williams, B&H Books, October 4, 2016.

Sidewalks on the Moon: A journey of a mystic architect through tradition, technology, and transformation, by Nader Khalili, Burning Gate Press, 1994.

Signals: How Questioning Assumptions Produces Smarter Decisions, by Dan Riordan, Post Hill Press, January 30, 2018.

Spider Woman Stories: Legends of the Hopi Indians, Selected and Interpreted by G.M. Mullett, University of Arizona Press, 1979.

Sum: Forty Tales From The Afterlives, David Eagleman, Vintage Books/Random House, 2009.

The 7 Habits of Highly Effective People: Restoring the Character Ethic, Powerful Lessons in Personal Change, by Stephen R. Covey, Franklin Covey Co., A Fireside Book, by Simon & Schuster, 1989.

The Botany of Desire: A plant's eye-view of the world, by Michael Pollan, Random House Trade Paperbacks, 2001.

The Consciousness Instinct: Unraveling the Mystery of How the Brain Makes the Mind, Michael S. Gazzaniga, Farrar, Straus and Giroux, April 3, 2018.

The Dip, by Seth Godin, Audible Studios, 04-27-07.
The Motivation Manifesto: A Declaration to Claim Your Personal Power, by Brendon Bruchard, Hayhouse Inc., 2014.

The Only Dance There Is, by Ram Dass, Anchor Books, 1974.

The Power of Now: A Guide to Spiritual Enlightenment, Eckhart Tolle, Namaste Publishing, August 19, 2004.

The Seven Spiritual Laws of Success: A Practical Guide to the Fulfillment of Your Dreams, by Deepak Chopra, Amber-Allen Publishing, 1993.

The Spontaneous Fulfillment of Desire: Harnessing the Infinite Power of Coincidence, by Deepak Chopra, Harmony Books, 2003.

The Top 10 Rules for Success: Rules to Succeed in Business and Life from Titans, Billionaires, & Leader who Changed the World, by Evan Carmichael, Evan Carmichael Communications Group, 2017.

The Travelers Gift: Seven Decisions That Determine Personal Success, by Andy Andrews, Nelson Books, 2002.

The Truth About Leadership: The No-fads, to the Heart-of-the-Matter Facts You Need to Know, By: James Kouzes, Barry Posner, Jossey-Bass, August 16, 2010.

Unfu*k Yourself: Get Out of Your Head and into Your Life, by Gary John Bishop, HarperAudio, August 1, 2017.

"Dragon Looking in my Window"
by Angel Lilly, 2019

Gabrielle Angel Dee Lilly

Some others who swayed me on this quest:
Alan Watts
Amanda Palmer
Andy Andrews
Anna Akana
Bill Burr
Bill Hicks
Bob Dylan
Chelsea Handler
Chris Cornell
Christie Marie Sheldon
Dandapani
Dave Chappell
David Letterman
Deepak Chopra
Doug Stanhope
Eddie Murphy
Elon Musk
Eric McFadden
Eckhart Tolle
Esther Hicks
Esther Perel
Evan Carmichael
Gabrielle Berstein
Gabrielle Reese
Gabrielle Roth
Gary Vaynerchuck
George Carlin
Gilbert Gottfried
Henry Rollins
Iliza Shlesinger
Jack Canfield
Jack White
Jason Silva
Jay Alan Samit
Jay Leno

Jay Shetty
Jessa Reed
Jim Jefferies
Jim Kwik
Jimmy Fallon
Joan Rivers
Joe Rogan
John Cleese
John Stewart
JP Seers
Kevin Hart
Layla Martin
Lilly Singh
Lily Ma
Lisa Bilyeu
Lisa Nichols
Les Claypool
Lewis Howes
Logic
Marie Forleo
Marisa Peers
Mike Dooley
Nader Khalili
Naveen Jain
Nick Cave
Oscar Wild
Peter Diamandis
Preston Smiles
Ralph Smart
Richard Branson
Rob Breszny
Rob Dyrdek
Robin Williams
Russell Brand
Sarah Silverman
Seth Godin

Gabrielle Angel Dee Lilly

Sophia Sundari
Sorelle Amore
Steve Jobs
Sun Ray Kelly
Tenacious D
Tiffany Haddish
Tim Ferriss
Tom Bilyeu
Tony Robbins
Vishen Lakhiani
Wayne Dyer
Whitney Cummings
Zig Ziglar

"DragonFly Swims By"
by Angel Lilly January 2019

Potential Playlist:

This is a list of songs that resonate with me at as resonating with this book in some way, at the time of publishing this. I aim to keep an active playlist on YouTube, which will probably continue to evolve over time, or it will die, as is the way of all things. For fun! For freedom!

4 Non Blondes - What's Up, t9
Alef - Sol
All Them Witches - Internet
alt-J - Left Hand Free
Anderson.Paak - Come Down, t4
Angel Lilly - Begin Again t27
Angel Lilly - Make Yourself, t4
Angel Lilly - Not One Way, t22
Band of Skulls - Navigate, t34
Beastie Boys - She's Crafty, t24
Black Sabbath - Faeries Wear Boots
Blind Willie Johnson - Nobody's Fault But Mine
Blondie - One Way Or Another
Blue Oyster Cult - Godzilla
Blue Oyster Cult - Burnin' For You
Bob Dylan - Simple Twist Of Fate
Bob Dylan - Tangled Up In Blue
Bob Dylan - Things Have Changed
Bob Marley - Trench Town Rock
Cage the Elephant - Trouble
Camper Van Beethoven - Oh Death
Concrete Blond - Free, t1
Crosby, Stills & Nash - Guinnevere, p10
David Bowie - Let's Dance
David Bowie - Rebel Rebel, t6
Dire Straits - Sultans Of Swing t28
Donovan - Happiness Runs, t42
Donovan - Season of the Witch, p17

DWIG - Orange Evening // Laut & Luise
Elton John - Goodbye Yellow Brick Road, t26
Eurythmics - Sweet Dreams t27
Fatboy Slim - Weapon Of Choice, t10
Fkj & Masego - Tadow
Fleetwood Mac - Oh Well/Peter Green
Flume & Chet Faker - Drop the Game
Frankie Goes to Hollywood - Relax, t26
Freedom - Django Unchained
Gorillaz - Clint Eastwood, t30
Hugo Kant - In The Woods
HU - Wolf totem
Irma Thomas - Anyone Who Knows What Love Is, t46
IZ - Over the rainbow
Jamiroquai - Virtual Insanity
Kenny Rogers - The Gambler, t40
Leonard Cohen - How the light gets in, t44
Led Zeppelin - When the Levee Breaks
Let's Get Ready to Rumble - Jock Jams (Start)
Lou Reed - Walk on the Wild Side
Morcheeba - Part Of The Process - Big Calm, t15
Nick Cave & The Bad Seeds - Red Right Hand
Pearl Jam - Do the Evolution, t2
Peter Gabriel - Sledgehammer
Pharrell Williams - Happy, t47
Pixies - Where Is My Mind
Portulgal. The Man - Live in the Moment
Primus - Southbound Pachyderm
Prince - Kiss
Queen - Bohemian Rhapsody, t15
Queens of the Stone Age - The Vampyre of Time & Memory
Queens of the Stone Age - Make It Wit Chu (Remix)
Nirvana - Smells Like Teen Spirit
Red Rider - Lunatic Fringe, t44
Ricky Martin - Livin' La Vida Loca, t39
Rising Appalachia - Scale Down

Gabrielle Angel Dee Lilly

Savages - You're My Chocolate
Sia - Alive
Simon & Garfunkel - The Sounds of Silence, t32
Steely Dan - Do It Again
Stevie Wonder - Superstition
Sugartooth - Seven & Seven
Supergiant - Everyman, t8
Tash Sultana - Welcome to the Jungle
ThaMuseMeant - Sweet Things, t17
The Avalanches - Because I'm Me
The Beatles – Blackbird, t23
The Beatles – Come Together
The Black Keys - I Got Mine
The Dead Weather - 60 Feet Tall
The Dead Weather - I Feel Love
The Doors - Twentieth Century Fox, t21
The Heavy - How You Like Me Now?
The Kills - Heart Of A Dog
The Revivalists - Wish I Knew You
The Rolling Stones - Sympathy For The Devil
The Smiths - How Soon Is Now?
The Ting Tings - That's Not My Name
The White Stripes - Ball and Biscuit
Tito & Tarantula - Strange Face, t26
Tom Waits - Gun Street Girl
Van Morrison - Tupelo Honey, t3
Wax Tailor - "The Games You Play"
Wax Tailor - Say Yes, t45
White Zombie - More Human Than Human
Zero 7 - Futures
Zero 7 - Somersault, t14
Zero 7 - The Space Between

Favorite Questions for clearer truths:
If not now, when?
Is that really true?
What do I really want?
How much does it matter right now?
What is trying to emerge?
What would love do?
Why do I really want this?
Is this what I really want?
You know you're driving, right?
What am I getting from this?
What is the greatest expression of myself I can be right now?
What happens next?

Go. Sit in your truthbox. Step out of your truthcube. Take your truthpill. Make your own truthpie.

Gabrielle Angel Dee Lilly

"Dragons' Watch"
by Angel Lilly, 2019

Your Personal Invitation:

Darling Reader,
This is not the end, though we may
pretend.

Begin Again.

Come outside and play.

Love,
A

Gabrielle Angel Dee Lilly

"Self Portrait, Down the Rabbit Hole"
by Angel Lilly, January 2019

"Change is afoot.
Comfort is still two socks. "
~ G. A. Lilly

Gabrielle Angel Dee Lilly

"Dragonheart Through the Looking Glass"
by Angel Lilly, January 2019

Gabrielle Angel Dee Lilly

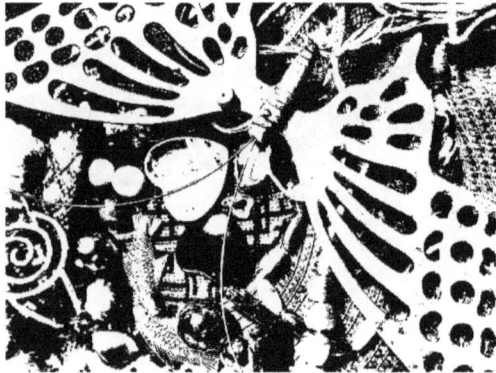

"Parts of Me"
by Angel Lilly, December 2018

"You can see my house from here."
By Angel Lilly, December 2018

www.ingramcontent.com/pod-product-compliance
Lightning Source LLC
Chambersburg PA
CBHW021501090426
42739CB00007B/406